WHO HOLDS THE KEY TO YOUR HEART?

WHO HOLDS THE KEY TO YOUR HEART?

LYSA TERKEURST

MOODY PRESS
CHICAGO

ISBN: 0-8024-3310-3

Printed in the United States of America
1 3 5 7 9 10 8 6 4 2

Dedicated to you, my friend.
My prayer is that this book will be the map
that leads you straight to the heart of God.
May you be able to lay down whatever burdens you are carrying
or hurts that still haunt you
and finally rejoice in God's amazing love.

CONTENTS

FOREWORD

The Christian life is a journey littered with obstacles and opportunities. It is a continuing path of discovery. Tiny little hands explore the miracle of their own natural bodies as babies become aware of themselves. Self-absorption gives way to an awakening realization that they are only a part of a human community. The search for identity begins in the early teenage years, as does the struggle for the purpose and meaning of life. Possessing only a natural heritage, we begin to sense that something is missing.

Life begins to change as though some force outside ourselves is orchestrating events. Some are in the midst of a crisis, while others are searching for what they inherently know is missing. Suddenly God becomes more than an abstract thought. He becomes our Father, and we are His children. We have a new family, a new heritage, and a new identity. We are children of God who are spiritually alive in Christ. The miracle of new birth has given us a new heart and a new spirit. Oh, the wonder of it all. The spiritual journey has just really begun as we seek to discover who our heavenly Father is and who we are in Christ.

The journey is intended to lead us to Christ and then take us on a path of growth so that we become more and more like Jesus. But there are obstacles along the way. The world system we were raised in becomes a hindrance to our self-discovery and growth. We are tempted to follow our old natural ways that are still ingrained in our minds. Not only that, the god of this world will continue to tempt, accuse, and deceive all those who have given their hearts to Christ. He can't do anything about our new identity and position in Christ, but if he can get us to believe that it isn't true, we will live as though it isn't. The world, the flesh, and the devil are enemies of our sanctification. If we give in to these obstacles, our journey will come to a standstill.

Before we came to Christ we had neither the presence of God in our lives nor the knowledge of His ways. So we all learned to live our lives independently of God. Mental strongholds were raised up against the knowledge of God, and we learned to defend ourselves. Then the miracle our new birth transferred us out of the kingdom of darkness and into the kingdom of God. We are no longer "in Adam;" we are "in Christ." Since we are new creations in Christ, old things have passed away and all things have become new. But why then do we still struggle with some of the old issues and thoughts? Because nobody pushed the delete button in our memory bank. Everything that was programmed into our minds is still there. That is why we must no longer be conformed to this world but be transformed by the renewing of our minds (Romans 12:2).

The continuing good news on this journey is that we have forces far greater working within us to ensure that we will be victorious. We just need to know what the nature of the battle is and how to win it. Lysa TerKeurst knows who she is in Christ, and she has come a long way on this journey of life. She knows well the battle for our minds and why we have to take every thought captive to the obedience of Christ. The fruit of the spirit is the result of the Holy Spirit working through our new hearts. She will show you how to win this battle for your mind, and, by the grace of God, you shall overcome the evil one, because in reality he can't touch us (1 John 5:18). May the peace of Christ rule in your hearts as you let the words of Christ richly dwell within you.

Dr. Neil T. Anderson
President Emeritus of Freedom In Christ Ministries

BEFORE YOU BEGIN

Before you begin reading, purchase a journal (if you don't already have one) to answer the questions you'll find throughout the text. You don't have to buy an expensive journal—a spiral notebook will do. Please don't skip over these exercises. Writing out your thoughts helps you work through your feelings and will provide a record of your growth over time. When you finish the book, you may want to go back and read over your journal entries to see where God has been leading you. If you faithfully recorded your thoughts in your journal, you'll be amazed at the healing God has done in your life.

This book can be used either individually or with a group. At the end of each chapter are group discussion questions. If you are participating in a group, these will be the focus of your discussion time. If you have time, jot down your thoughts about these questions before your meeting; that way you'll have a written reminder of what you learned in the chapter. If you're not participating in a group, please be sure to answer these questions in your journal. They will greatly benefit you.

May God bless you as you move from bondage to freedom and healing!

ACKNOWLEDGMENTS

O f all the books I've written, this one has reminded me most of all the people who have helped me understand the healing power of Jesus Christ. Many have come alongside me and loved me to the point where I was finally able to accept God's forgiveness and rejoice in His amazing love.

First, and foremost, Jesus, thank You for loving me enough to never give up on me. I can't wait to see You face-to-face and dance with You in heaven.

To the love of my life, Art—you are my knight in shining armor!

To Sharon Jaynes—thank you for reading me that letter from Baby Jaynes all those years ago. It brought me much comfort and healing to know your baby welcomed mine into Jesus' arms of love.

To Chris, Sharon TerKeurst (my mother-in-law), and all the ladies at the Charlotte Pregnancy Care Center and other counselors at Crisis Pregnancy Centers—your dedication is making a difference in the lives of many; you certainly changed mine.

To Sandy Day—thank you for teaching me how to find the victorious Christian life.

To all the thousands of women who've heard me share this message at conferences and retreats and who answered Jesus' offer of hope and healing— seeing God work miracles in your lives with the ashes of my past has brought such joy to my life.

*To Sheila Mangum—*I couldn't have written this book without your encouragement and support. Thank you for your creative ideas and endless hours of reviewing the manuscript.

*To Liz Duckworth, Kathy Davis, and Julie Küss—*thank you for going through my manuscript with a fine-tooth comb and getting all the tangles out.

*To Mark Maddox, Yvette Maher, and the entire Renewing the Heart team—*thank you for believing this is a message worth sharing.

*To my entire staff at Proverbs 31 Ministries—*your dedication amazes me. Thank you for the privilege of working with you.

*To the members of South Brook Community Church—*thank you for your input and excitement for this project. What a blessing to teach it to you first.

And last, but certainly not least, to the three girls who call me Mommy— thanks for making my life more fun than I ever thought it could be!

INTRODUCTION

*A solemn consideration, when I enter a great city by night,
that every one of those darkly clustered houses encloses its own secret;
every beating heart in the hundreds of thousands of breasts there is,
in some of its imaginings, a secret to the heart nearest it.*

·❖·

CHARLES DICKENS

It wasn't in the middle of my busy days that I was particularly aware of the problem. It was when my body stilled, my guard let down, and my mind tried to rest that a sharp, piercing pain in my heart consumed me. Anxiety and guilt stirred and churned until I burst forth in a flood of tears. Somehow those heartfelt sobs helped take the edge off my pain for a little while.

Sometimes I became so emotionally drained that sleep would finally overtake my weary body and I could escape for a time. Then I would awaken, and for a few sleepy seconds I was free until reality rushed in. Being fully awake meant being fully aware of all that held me captive.

I was a prisoner indeed. Shame had given me a life sentence. Despair was my only future. Fear erected bars in my prison cell of loneliness. I had very few visitors, but those who did visit were worse than no company at all. Discontentment would come to remind my heart of what could have been. Insecurity would come to tell me I was worthless and deserved to be in this place. Doubt would bring with him whispers that God had never and would never care about me. Bitterness was the only meal to feast on and addiction my only pleasure. It was a miserable existence, and no escape seemed possible. I reasoned that I deserved this life sentence and nothing better.

Maybe some version of my story reflects the condition of your own heart as you read these words. Well, you have not chosen this book by accident. This is your divine appointment. Your soul has been drawn by the God of the universe to a place of hope and healing. He directed and orchestrated all of His creation to bring you to a place of mercy.

Rest assured, my friend, inside most hearts exists a secret place. Behind a door of hidden thoughts and painful memories brews a hurt so overwhelming it can't be allowed to surface. The slightest peek inside reveals insecurities better left alone. So the door is locked and secrets are kept even from God. Or are they?

The truth is God knows the secrets of your heart and He wants them. The maker of this vast and wonderful universe is waiting for the key to the heart of His greatest creation—you. He wants the key to your heart, your whole heart, especially the hidden parts.

When you hold this key, Satan will wrestle it from you, unlock your shame, and use it to accuse and condemn you. He loves to keep a person in such a defeated state of mind that she becomes totally ineffective for the cause of Christ. The irony is that the very things you consider shameful can be used by God for His glory.

This is the beauty of Christ's death and resurrection. The price has been paid and your slate wiped clean. There is no sin too big to keep you from the touch of the Master's hand. God is still in the miracle business, and He wants the key to your heart.

I've lived the message in these pages, and God has walked every amazing step of my life with me. As a matter of fact, it was He who carried me so that I could continue and not grow weary. He led me over the great divide from a place of darkness into the light my soul longed for.

Your soul longs for the light too. The last thing you need is another book to tell you that this place of light exists. You believe that a wonderful life filled with love and laughter is possible, but your heart hasn't known how to find it. Or, worse yet, you've felt unworthy even to dream of this place, much less journey there. Well, think of this book as more than ink, paper, and glue. It is your map through the deepest places of your heart, where God can reveal His truth and set you free.

You are more than worthy to go to this place. You were made for this place, a place of pure freedom. This is where shame's sentence is stamped with love's seal: "Pardoned and released." This is where despair gives way to joy and fear can no longer hold you back from peace. Your prison cell of loneliness crumbles, and God gives you kindness in its place. There are no more visits from discontentment, insecurity, and doubt. God's truth of patience, goodness, and faithfulness are your companions now. You no longer crave bitterness to satisfy your desire for revenge. God is your avenger, so now your desire is for gentle forgiveness. And the addictions that once enticed you are no longer the longings of your heart. Your greatest desire is to pursue the great Lover of your soul.

Is this really possible? Yes! How will God do this? By revealing Himself and His truth.

Truth is the key that unlocks the chains Satan has twisted around your heart. In John 8:31–32 Jesus says, "If you hold to my teaching, you are really my disciples. Then you will know the truth, and the truth will set you free." You see, you have been deceived by the Father of Lies. John 8:44 says, "He [Satan] was a murderer from the beginning, not holding to the truth, for there is no truth in him."

Did you catch those words: "no truth"? That means absolutely none at all. Not even a trace of truth. All these years he's been whispering in your ear, deceiving you, and then slamming condemnation down on you like a heavy prison door. Well, we are about to open that door—to fling it open.

We will give Jesus the key to our hearts and let Him unlock every hurting and dark place. He will then offer us hope, heal us with God's Word, and fill us with His redeeming light. Don't be discouraged if this doesn't happen overnight. Healing is often a process.

When you know God's truth and His truth penetrates your darkness, it will set you free! When Satan tries to entice you to step back into fear, loneliness, discontentment, insecurity, doubt, bitterness, and addictions, you'll have God's Word to shine truth on your situation. The truth clearly reminds us that God loves us, He'll never leave us, and we always have tremendous hope in Him.

I love the story in John 8:3–11, which tells of a woman caught in adultery by the teachers and Pharisees. They brought her in front of a crowd where Jesus was teaching and threw her at His feet. They were ready to stone her to death, but Jesus stopped them in their tracks with His reply: "If any one of you is without sin, let him be the first to throw a stone at her" (v. 7).

In verses 9–10 we read, "At this, those who heard began to go away one at a time, the older ones first, until only Jesus was left, with the woman still standing there. Jesus straightened up and asked her, 'Woman where are they? Has no one condemned you?'"

This is the place where you and I come in. We must step into this woman's shoes with whatever sins and circumstances we carry and answer Jesus' question for ourselves. Jesus is looking at us with eyes of love and compassion, ready to reveal this significant truth to us. At this point it is up to each of us to decide whether to turn and run back to our familiar prison cells or to grasp the hand of truth and start anew. Imagine how Jesus' face expresses His anticipation as He asks the question only you can answer: "Has no one condemned you?"

"No one, sir."

Oh, can't you feel the excitement in the air? Can't you see the sheer joy in Jesus' eyes? This is the answer He has waited so long to comfort you with. This is the reason He came, suffered, and died for you. Now, finally, the time has come for Him to speak directly to your soul. All of creation seems to pause as He speaks. This is not a whisper or even just a reply. No, the Bible says that Jesus declared, "Then neither do I condemn you. . . . Go now and leave your life of sin" (v. 11).

✏ *Pull out your journal and record your thoughts here. Write your own name in this verse: "Then neither do I condemn [your name]."*

The break in the text lets us know that Jesus paused here. I can't help but wonder if it was because He was so full of emotion that His heart could hardly contain all He was feeling. But this is not where the story ends—far from it.

You see, this is where our adventure begins. For after Jesus paused, He spoke to the people again, saying, "I am the light of the world. Whoever follows me will never walk in darkness, but will have the light of life" (v. 12).

This is where we start. Now we go and sin no more. Not that we won't trip and fall into sin ever again—we will still stumble at times. But never again will we grope in the darkness. Here we see the light and follow after it wholeheartedly. For He has promised that He will not condemn us for our pasts but will carry us into the future. Let His Word bathe your soul. Drink these words in and let them saturate the deepest parts of your heart.

And so our journey begins.

✏ *Record these words in your journal: "I am the light of the world. Whoever follows me will never walk in darkness, but will have the light of life" (John 8:12). What hope does the light of life give you?*

DISCUSSION QUESTIONS

1. Do you think most people hide secrets in their hearts? Why?

2. What can we do to make this group a safe place for someone to reveal her secrets, should she choose to do so?

3. What danger is there in hiding secrets in the darkness?

4. What hope can be found in bringing our deep hurts and secrets out into the light?

5. What sweet hope did Jesus offer the woman in John 8?

6. What does it mean to be condemned? How does it make you feel to know that you are not condemned?

CHAPTER ONE

SHAME IS SATAN'S SIGNATURE
LOVE IS GOD'S REPLY

I sought the LORD, and he answered me; he delivered me from all my fears.
Those who look to him are radiant; their faces are never covered with shame.

·❖·

PSALM 34:4–5

I still remember the outdated furniture and stale coldness of that room. Women from all walks of life were there, and forever they and I would have something in common. Our paths had crossed at this awful place, a place where life was exchanged for death. We would now share an unmentionable secret that would shake some of us to the very foundations of our lives.

I wish I could say I was concerned about the others there and reached out to help, but I was consumed with my own crisis. No one let her eyes meet another's. Though medical fluorescents brightly lit the room, the heavy darkness in my soul made true vision nearly impossible.

What had brought me to this place? Certainly I had people to blame. There was the man who sexually abused me in childhood. Was I still that little girl who felt trapped by his threats and abuse? I remembered standing in the only room in his house where I could have escaped through a small window in a bathroom with a high ceiling. Though I stretched with all my eight-year-old might, I could not reach the window. For three years the abuse continued. I never grew tall enough to reach that window.

I could blame my biological father. Maybe if he had given me the love and acceptance I so desperately longed for, I would not have come to this place. Why had he abandoned our family? In my second year of high school, my dad had called the social services department of Florida and reported that he had raped me during one of our weekend visits. I felt broken, rejected, and ashamed. Why had my dad said those things? They were not true. What was so wrong with me that my own dad would reject me in such a shameful way? My own father couldn't even love me; what made me think any other man ever could?

I could blame God. Why had a loving God let such terrible things happen to me? Why had he let my baby sister die after I begged and pleaded for her healing? Why didn't He just wave His majestic hand and fix all that was broken in my life? Where was He? Why did He leave me all alone?

Tears filled my eyes and deep sobs poured from my soul in that cold room. I knew I could not blame anyone but myself. I'd walked into this place. I'd signed the papers. I'd allowed my baby to be aborted.

SHAME IS SATAN'S SIGNATURE

Satan, sin, shame. You can almost hear the slithering beast hissing at the mention of these words. They blend together in their pronunciation and work together in the destruction of all that lies in their wake. I can just imagine Satan slithering close to an unsuspecting victim, hissing enticing words that lead to sin and then boastfully signing his name across the victim's heart: *Shame.*

Satan bursts out laughing as his devastated prey is left to piece together a broken heart.

Webster's New World Dictionary defines shame as "a painful feeling of guilt for improper behavior." I can identify with this definition because I have felt shame's pain—a deep, constant throbbing of regret from the past mixed with dread of the future.

Shame consumes you. It overwhelms you. You try to run from it but quickly realize there is no escape. So you accept the mark shame has placed on you, while trying to hide it and pretend it's not there. It is an age-old feeling that has plagued every human God ever created. As a matter of fact, it is the first negative emotion recorded. Let's look at the first time shame made his debut.

Adam and Eve were living an amazing life. They were surrounded by beauty and plenty. They lived in a lush garden, had all the delicious food they could ever want, and had an incredible marriage. There was no sin, and as Genesis 2:25 says, "The man and his wife were both naked, and they felt no shame."

Then the craftiest of all the creatures slithered onto the scene and set out to deceive Eve. He first questioned her about what God had instructed. "Did God really say, 'You must not eat from any tree in the garden'?" (Genesis 3:1), making her doubt the validity of God's instructions. Eve replied that God said they must not eat (true) or even touch (not true) the fruit of the tree of the knowledge of good and evil, or they would die (v. 3).

But Satan twisted God's truth and answered, "You will not surely die. . . . For God knows that when you eat of it your eyes will be opened, and you will be like God, knowing good and evil" (vv. 4–5).

Do you see why Satan is called crafty? The root word from the original Hebrew for "craftiest" is *'aram,* which means "to form a cunning plan." Mustering all the skill he possessed, Satan contrived a well-thought-through plan to deceive Eve into sin.

His tactics are the same when Satan deceives us today. "Did

God *really* say that sex before marriage is wrong? Surely something that feels so right can't be wrong, now can it? It's a good thing to experience the ultimate expression of love before you are married. If you don't, how can you be certain he's the right partner? Isn't this something you want to know before making that lifelong commitment? Hisssss, hisssss, hissssss."

Then, just like Eve, we let Satan's lies enter our minds and we rationalize our way into shame's grasp. Genesis 3:6–7 records the tragic fall of man (comments added).

> *When the woman saw that the fruit of the tree was good for food* [first rationalization: I have to eat] *and pleasing to the eye* [second rationalization: surely something that looks this good can't be bad], *and also desirable for gaining wisdom* [third rationalization: it is a good thing to want to be like God—three strikes and you're out], *she took some and ate it. She also gave some to her husband, who was with her, and he ate it* [they sinned]. *Then the eyes of both of them were opened* [they moved from rationalization to realization], *and they realized they were naked* [shame grabs his victim]; *so they sewed fig leaves together and made coverings for themselves.*

We've been trying to cover shame's mark ever since.

Not only do we try to cover our sins, but we also mimic Adam and Eve's attempt to hide from God. Verse 8 tells us that "they hid from the LORD God among the trees of the garden." But God never leaves us in this hiding place long. He looks for us, calls us to "come out, come out, wherever you are."

This is exactly what God did for Adam and Eve: "The LORD God called to the man, 'Where are you?'" (v. 9). You can almost hear the heartbreak in the Creator's voice as He cries, "My beloved creation, why, why? I gave you everything and you could not honor My one request. Oh, if only you knew what you've done. If only you could see all the tears that will come as a result of this tragic mistake. If only you knew what I will have to sacrifice to bring you back to everlasting life."

God confronted Adam and Eve and told them the consequences of their sins. There are always consequences to our sins, and often they are deeper than is obvious at first. God said, "For dust you are and to dust you will return" (v. 19).

Interestingly enough, when I looked up the Hebrew word for dust I found the word *'aphar,* which contains "ashes" as part of its definition. Our bodies literally die and turn to dust as a natural part of the decaying process. This is just the opposite of our experience in Isaiah 61:3, where a different Hebrew word is translated *ashes* to tell that when we grieve, God can comfort our hearts by bestowing on us "a crown of beauty instead of ashes."

I also know firsthand how God can take what Satan meant for shame and use it for His glory. Think of it this way: Just when we think we've messed up so badly that our lives are nothing but heaps of ashes, God pours His Living Water over us and mixes the ashes into clay. He then takes this clay and molds it into a vessel of beauty. After He fills us with His overflowing love, He can use us to pour His love into the hurting lives of others.

The story ends with a reminder that even though God can redeem our sins, sin always separates us from God's best. Sin's consequences could not let Adam and Eve stay in Paradise. They were banished from the Garden of Eden. But love would not let God abandon Adam and Eve. Genesis 3:21 is so precious. It says, "The LORD God made garments of skin for Adam and his wife and clothed them."

I can just imagine God gently removing Adam and Eve's frail little fig leaves and saying, "Don't disguise your shame with inadequate coverings. I will make a good covering for you. It's not to hide your shame as the fig leaves, for we have already revealed your sin and dealt with it. This is the protective covering of a sacrificed animal."

Sin demands a sacrifice. God knew that this time the shed blood of animals would be shame's sacrifice, but one day that sacrifice would require precious blood dripping from a cross.

LOVE IS GOD'S REPLY

Here we stand at the foot of the Cross. Love has made the ultimate and final sacrifice. His red blood drips onto our shame, and this is where the miracle occurs.

Does love's blood add to the stain, making the guilt of our shame grow? No. Love's red blood pours onto shame's stain and washes it pure white. In Isaiah 1:18 God says, "Though your sins are like scarlet, they shall be as white as snow; though they are red as crimson, they shall be like wool."

In the original, the word for the red mentioned here is *'adam,* which means "dyed red." This word is very similar to a Hebrew term for mankind, which we see in the name Adam. God knew even before Adam was created and named that he would fall into sin and be dyed red—and that only the shed blood of His Son could wipe man's slate clean—yet He still chose to create us.

This is love's reply: "For God so loved the world that he gave his one and only Son, that whoever believes in him shall not perish but have eternal life. For God did not send his Son into the world to condemn the world, but to save the world through him" (John 3:16–17). Note that it does not say, "For God had pity on us," or even, "God felt obligated." No, it was love that nailed His Son to that tree. Love, my friend. Agape love. Pure, unfathomable, unconditional love for you and me.

Make no mistake, love's reply was not just to forgive us and bring us back into eternal fellowship with God, though surely this would have been enough. Love went one step further to show us the depth of His care and compassion. First Peter 2:24 reveals something more to us: "He himself [Jesus] bore our sins in his body on the tree, so that we might die to sins and live for righteousness; by his wounds *you have been healed*" (italics added). Not only are we forgiven, not only is our relationship with God eternally restored, but we are healed!

This is shame's defeat. This is the end of his story. This is where he exits the stage of our lives, never to appear again. As a matter of fact, his name is wiped from the program as if he had never even slithered into the play at all. Can anyone give me an "Amen" right here?

So we know we are healed, but our human minds compel us to ask how. Never fear, my friend; love has an answer. It occurs in that same passage of 2 Peter. Let's read it again: "He Himself [Jesus] bore our sins in his body on the tree, so that we might die to sins and live for righteousness; *by his wounds* you have been healed" (italics added).

Now we have to walk back to the Cross. There we see Jesus' wounds: The pierced hands and feet, the gashes on His head from a thorny crown, the bruises and cuts from merciless beatings, and the swollen lips from extreme thirst.

In John 19:31–34, two amazing truths are revealed about Jesus' wounds. First, verse 31 tells us that the soldiers had been instructed to break the legs of those crucified and remove their bodies in preparation for a special Sabbath. Crucified men would be an eyesore for their religious holiday, so the religious leaders wanted the men dead and gone. When a person was crucified, excessive pressure on the diaphragm made it extremely difficult to breathe. So a person being crucified would push himself up with his legs to catch his breath. Breaking his legs would prevent him from catching his breath, resulting in death.

We learn in verse 32 that the legs of the two men crucified with Jesus were broken and their bodies taken down. Then in verse 33 we learn that they did not break Jesus' legs because He was already dead. The point that Jesus' legs were not broken is significant, for it meant that the Scriptures would be fulfilled even in this detail of Jesus' crucifixion. We know from prophecies in Exodus 12:46; Numbers 9:12; and Psalm 34:20 that "not one of his bones will be broken" (John 19:36).

The first truth about Jesus' wounds is that Scripture will be fulfilled even if it is at the hands of evil. Nothing can alter God's plan. Isaiah 54:10 says, "'Though the mountains be shaken and the hills be removed, yet my unfailing love for you will not be shaken nor my covenant of peace be removed,' says the LORD, who has compassion on you."

Nothing shakes God and makes Him change His mind midstream. God does not forget His promises. Not even seeing His Son die for people who cursed Him and spat upon Him could make God forget His love for us. God had said that not one bone would be broken and none was.

So let me ask you, in light of this profound truth, if God does not condemn you, are you condemned? No, as we stand here at this old rugged cross and feel His Son's blood washing us clean, we cannot deny love this victory.

Now, just to make sure love is allowed a triumphant processional, we move on to a second truth gleaned from Jesus' wounds. John 19:34 says, "Instead [of breaking his legs], one of the soldiers pierced Jesus' side with a spear, bringing a sudden flow of blood and water."

I was once in a Sunday school class in which the teacher focused on this passage. In doing extensive medical research she found that the only way a person's side would pour forth both blood and water was if his heart literally broke apart and burst open. Now, I do not know all the physical ramifications of this medical claim, but I do know "When in doubt, check God's Word." To do this we turn back to Psalm 22, where David prophesied Christ's crucifixion.

In verse 16 we read of His hands and feet being pierced. Verse 18 tells of His garments being divided and lots being cast for His clothing. And in verse 14 we learn of the condition of His heart: "I am poured out like water, and all my bones are out of joint. My heart has turned to wax; it has melted away within me." This takes my breath away. Christ died of a broken heart! Yes, the soldiers beat Him and nailed Him to the cross, but it was my sin that broke His heart and killed Him. It was His love for me that kept Him there until death.

That's why we had to walk back to the Cross. You see, this was not just an event that happened two thousand years ago, something we read about as history. No, we were there. Jesus saw shame's ugly mark on all of us. Yes, you and me. He saw Lysa TerKeurst sitting in that abortion clinic and knew she would need the healing only His wounds . . . only His death . . . only His love could give her! He also thought of you as He hung there on that cross. He could have called down a legion of angels to rescue Him, but His love for you kept Him there. Don't deny that by His wounds, you are healed. Jesus paid the ransom with His love. Now give to love what is due: shame's captive.

✏ *It is your choice. You know love's truth. Write in your journal these three truths:*

1. By His wounds, I am healed.

2. God never forgets His promises. When He says that nothing I have ever done could make Him stop loving me, it is absolute truth. His love for me cannot be shaken.

3. Jesus died of a broken heart so that I don't have to. He thought of me on that cross, and because of His sacrifice, I am forgiven and set free.

Psalm 44:21 tells us that God knows the secrets of our hearts. He does know them, but He wants us to release them to Him and His healing truth.

✏ *In your journal record whatever is heavy on your heart. Write your hurts out, and ask God for forgiveness for your sins and for healing today.*

Releasing your pain in this way and letting God's truth be the healing balm that settles over your wounds will set you free from shame forever. Yes, sin's consequences may still remain, but remember that God can bring good even from sin's ashes. It all comes down to repentance and being willing to turn and walk away from shame.

Oh, shame will reach for you and try to recapture you, but the arm of the Lord is longer still. Romans 8:37–39 proclaims,

No, in all these things we are more than conquerors through him who loved us. For I am convinced that neither death nor life, neither angels nor demons, neither the present nor the future, nor any powers, neither height nor depth, nor anything else in all creation, will be able to separate us from the love of God that is in Christ Jesus our Lord.

The Lord will take you where shame's touch can no longer be felt. Now, when you stumble over sin's rocks in the road, you'll get up. You'll feel the Master's touch as you ask Him to forgive you and He wipes you clean. You'll smile as you look for shame's old marks and all you see is love's stamp: "Forgiven and set free."

Love has provided you with your true identity. You are a child of God, holy and dearly loved.

✏ *Write in your journal about how you have always viewed yourself. Now write out Ephesians 1:4–5, "For he chose us in him before the creation of the world to be holy and blameless in his sight. In love he predestined us to be adopted as his sons through Jesus Christ, in accordance with his pleasure and will."*

God holds you up high for all the world to see, and He declares, "This one is Mine, forever and ever. No longer is she defeated and conquered, for through Me and My love, she is a conqueror!"

"Through the unfailing love of the Most High he will not be shaken" (Psalm 21:7).

A HEART RENEWED

It was the day I had dreamed about all my life. I was surrounded by all those I loved. My dress made me feel like a princess, and the church and reception hall never looked more beautiful. But as the church doors opened and everyone stood as I entered, my heart was broken. I pressed my bouquet against my chest, hoping no one would see the shame I had buried there. You see, just a few months earlier, I had learned I was pregnant.

I was terrified to go to my friends at church for fear of becoming an outcast. *After all,* I wrongly reasoned, *if people discover I'm not perfect, then I can't be a Christian.*

I knew well the sting of rejection and decided to go where I wouldn't be judged. So I went to an abortion clinic and was told the procedure would be quick, easy, and that I'd never think about it again. I bought their horrible lie and had an abortion.

The moment I awoke from the anesthesia, I knew I'd regret this decision for the rest of my life. The shame and guilt overwhelmed me.

Now, here I was, promising to love another when I so desperately hated myself. No one but me knew about the uninvited guest who was there. Shame stole the show on my wedding day.

Not long after we returned home from our honeymoon, all the guilt and pain from our mistakes began to haunt us. Our marriage was falling apart, and we both knew we needed help. After many counselors seemed unable to help us, one wise older pastor told us that he felt we needed to let God do a work in each of our hearts as individuals; then God would knit our hearts back together.

Finally, I found out about a post-abortion Bible study at the local crisis pregnancy center. Every week my husband would drive me to a back entrance of the clinic where I would shamefully walk up a back staircase to meet with my counselor. I was so afraid someone might see me that I would not take a chance on parking my car at the center.

One day my husband couldn't drive me to the center. I don't remember exactly what happened, but just before I reached the center, I ran into the back of the car in front of me. As the man in the other car approached my crumpled vehicle, I fixed my eyes on his wild blond hair. He never concerned himself with his car; rather, he came up to me, asked if I was all right, and told me not to worry about his car. Then he instructed me to get where I was going, and as quickly as the accident happened, he was gone.

Now, I don't know if you've ever encountered an angel, but I think I had a car accident with one! I knew at that point that God had not left me and that somehow everything was going to be all right. Somewhere in the midst of the sound of car engines, I was almost certain I'd heard the brush of an angel's wings.

I drove up to the center that day and parked right in front. There in that Bible study I met a God I'd never known before. I learned a lot about God's character. We read in the Scriptures that God is a loving God who would forgive and who could heal the hurts of His people. The process was slow and painful, but as I dealt with the abortion, my heart felt hope for the first time.

Soon afterward I made some wonderful discoveries in Scripture: I am a holy and dearly loved child of God; He is my heavenly Father; nothing can separate me from His love; He sent His Son, Jesus, to die on a cross so that I could be forgiven and have my slate wiped clean. (We'll look at these Scriptures later in the book.)

For years, whenever I looked in the mirror, all I could see was an abused, rejected little girl who'd turned her back on God when she couldn't understand Him. Then she'd had an abortion and thought that was one sin for which there was no forgiveness. But that's not what God saw. He saw a dearly loved child, and He longed for fellowship with her. His heart broke for the things that caused her so much pain.

When I finally looked into God's Word and let Him be my mirror, I saw for the first time the truth of who I really am. The chains of bondage started to release their painful grip as I realized it was not *religion* that I needed but rather a *relationship*. That day I met two people. First, I met the Jesus I never really knew before. Even though I'd accepted Him into my heart some twenty years earlier, I had not pursued a personal relationship with Him. The second person I met was Lysa TerKeurst, a holy and dearly loved child of the Most High King, who was accepted and set free!

Soon after I came to understand my identity in Jesus, I was working on a Bible study that posed a very difficult question: Would I go wherever and do whatever God asked me to? At first I said yes, of course, and then I attempted to move on to the next question. Again and again my eyes were drawn back to the first question. God was making me examine more than just the question; I was also having to examine my heart.

You see, I felt God's call to share my testimony, but I was not willing. I told God that I would do whatever He desired except share my life story. I felt God impressing on my heart that I needed to trust Him, that He had plans to take what the devil meant for evil in my life and use it for His glory. A few weeks later I drove to a little country church where I had a speaking engagement. I told God that I would share my testimony just this time.

That day I witnessed a miracle of God. Tear-stained faces all over the room confirmed that this was a message people needed to hear. Over half the women in attendance recommitted their lives to Christ. As I drove home, I promised God that I would go wherever He called me to go and share my story—*our story.*

I don't know the events in your life. I don't know what hurts might haunt you. I don't know what secrets are in your heart, but God knows, and He's calling you to give them over to His healing touch. We all come to a critical place at one time or another where we must decide whether we will walk life's journey with God or without Him. There is no in-between. I chose God, and what He has done for me is truly miraculous.

It's called amazing love. He has filled me with His love, and that love now spills over into every area of my life. I am now able to love my husband. I am able to be the kind of mommy my three daughters deserve. My home is filled with joy. My friendships are characterized by an openness that fosters loving accountability. I can now extend my hands out into the community with the love of Christ. I can do all of this not because of my own strength but because of God working in me and through me.

I walk with Jesus every day. I seek His face on good days and bad. Now let me assure you, I still mess up. My dear sisters, not one of us is perfect. That's why we need a personal and ongoing relationship with the One who is.

Let me encourage you to start a new journey with God today. Pray and ask Him to draw near to you. Ask Him to reveal Himself to you like never before. Be faithful to read your Bible and journal verses through which God speaks to you. Lift every area of your life up to Him in prayer. Praise Him for His faithfulness. Thank Him for His goodness. Let Him guide your every step from here on out. Take His hand and trust His heart. He will never leave you, my friend. He loves you. Oh my, how He loves you![1]

DISCUSSION QUESTIONS

1. John 8:31–32 says, "If you hold to my teaching, you are really my disciples. Then you will know the truth, and the truth will set you free." What can the truth set us free from?

2. Is there any truth at all in Satan? What hope does this give us?

3. How does Satan use shame to defeat people?

4. What new truths did you learn about what Jesus did at the Cross?

5. Which of these truths had the greatest impact on you personally?

6. What should you do when you start feeling shame try to pull you back?

CHAPTER TWO

DESPAIR IS SATAN'S DESTINY
JOY IS GOD'S REPLY

He has sent me to bind up the brokenhearted,
to proclaim freedom for the captives
and release from darkness for the prisoners,
to proclaim the year of the LORD's favor
and the day of vengeance of our God,
to comfort all who mourn, and provide for those who grieve in Zion—
to bestow on them a crown of beauty instead of ashes,
the oil of gladness instead of mourning,
and a garment of praise instead of a spirit of despair.
They will be called oaks of righteousness, a planting of the LORD
for the display of his splendor.

·❖·

ISAIAH 61:1–3

When our second daughter, Ashley, was born, she appeared to be very healthy. We brought her home from the hospital and were overcome with the joy this little dark-headed person brought to our family. Her smile was captivating and her big brown eyes full of love. Though it was challenging to manage both a newborn and a sixteen-month-old, I felt incredibly blessed.

Then, as it had done so often in my life, tragedy struck. Ashley became seriously ill due to a rare protein allergy that put her in intensive care. Her condition continued to decline, and I grew more and more desperate. I wanted to shake my fist at God and scream with all my might that He could not have this child. I had already lost a sister, Haley, who was only sixteen months old when she died from complications from liver transplant surgery. I was in college when she died and will never forget the heartbreak of seeing this precious little one slip from our lives. I guess in some strange way, I felt as though Haley's death was my family's insurance policy against any other tragic death.

Now I knew Ashley was in real trouble. Her tiny body was wasting away, and her rosy coloring had turned nearly ash gray. It was no surprise when the intensive care doctor told my husband and me that her condition required immediate emergency surgery. He gently told us that the prognosis did not look promising, and he was not sure she would survive the procedure. He gave us five minutes to tell our sweet baby good-bye.

How do you tell a child good-bye? How do you hold a little innocent life you have promised to nurture and protect and tell her that you have to let her go? How does a mother let her dreams for her daughter's future vanish?

My mind flooded with thoughts of a future that ought to be: A two-year-old's spaghetti-smeared kiss and tickles and giggles and peek-a-boos. Packing her little backpack for her first day of kindergarten. Cheering for her as she played her favorite sport. Picking out a prom dress. Straightening her veil on her wedding day.

Despair gripped my heart, squeezing out every ounce of joy. *Where are You, God? Don't you hear my prayers?*

DESPAIR IS SATAN'S DESTINY

Sometimes despair makes a grand entrance, flaunting his presence in the face of tragedy: A woman miscarries. A teen is killed in a car accident. A husband is struck down by a heart attack in the prime of life. An entire family is murdered in their home. A woman is raped.

Despair has certainly made grand entrances in my life, though my experience with Ashley was the most heartrending of all. Like most mothers, I can deal with my own pain but not that of my children.

Instead of springing from a major event, despair sometimes creeps into life silently. The stress and demands of everyday life may beckon him. Perhaps, seeking to rediscover joy, a person holds out her empty cup and hopes someone will fill it. She watches her husband's cues and listens for words that might add something to her cup, an assurance that she is indeed a good wife. Then she holds out her cup to her children. *Am I a good mother?*, she wonders. Or she holds out her cup to her friend and watches and listens. *Am I a good friend?*

With each encounter she watches, listens, and waits. Sometimes she likes the cues she reads and the comments made. Other times she does not. She stares down into the cup, feeling frustrated at the apparent inability of anybody to fill her emptiness.

Satan whispers, "You're not a good wife. And you're not a good mother. And your friend doesn't really like you. She just puts up with you."

Satan wants you to walk down despair's path. It's his destiny, and he wants others to join him. Nothing Satan can do will change his eternal damnation, but he's not going quietly. He's like a snake with his head cut off whose body continues to thrash and whip about. His death is certain, but he won't go down without a destructive fight.

Philippians 3:18–19 says, "For, as I have often told you before and now say again even with tears, many live as enemies of the cross of Christ. Their destiny is destruction, their god is their stomach, and their glory is in their shame. Their mind is on earthly things."

You can hardly turn on the television today without being bombarded with "earthly" offers of happiness. Buy this car and you'll be happy. Have this burger your way and you'll be happy.

Feed your cat this cat chow and you'll see him do a little dance and . . . be happy!

Why do marketers pitch their products as the ultimate path to happiness? Because they know that each of us has a desperate desire for happiness. And this is no revelation. Even the founding fathers of our great nation wanted America to be a country of inalienable rights to life, liberty, and, yes, the pursuit of happiness.

Despite our focus on happiness, statistics indicate that America is actually a very unhappy society. To borrow from the words of Paul in Philippians 3, our minds seem to be "on earthly things." There is a disconnect in America's pursuit of happiness, and I think it's found in three little letters: j–o–y.

Do you think that happiness is the opposite of despair? Have you ever caught yourself trying hard to fill your life with things that provide a temporary happiness high, only to sink down a few days or even hours later? Could it be that the true key to unlocking the chains of despair is an unshakable, foundational joy?

✐ *What are some things you've thought would make you happy? Record these in your journal and note whether or not they actually gave you the lasting happiness you were looking for.*

You see, without joy, happiness will always elude us. Joy is a foundational assurance that is unchanging despite circumstances. Happiness can be tossed to and fro like a feather in the wind. Circumstances come and we're up. The winds of circumstances change, and suddenly we're plummeting down. Despair is waiting to catch us and wrap us up in arms of darkness and depression. We want so desperately for our cups to be filled, yet Jesus is the only One who promises enough Living Water to fill them. In fact, through Him, we will overflow with a consistent and peaceful joy.

Despair is not just a desperate lack of joy and hope for the future but rather a present state of mind. Ask anyone battling with despair and depression to describe his or her feelings, and you'll hear the word *darkness*. It's an eclipse of the mind, a dark shadow that covers and hides our rightful inheritance of joy for today. Make no mistake whose shadow this is. Satan loves to wait in the wings of life and throw his dark cape over an unsuspecting mind.

Jesus knew this darkness. When He took on the sins of the world, His Father could not look upon Him. God's holiness forced Him to turn His face and forsake His Son for the sins He bore in His body. Mark 15:33–34 says, "At the sixth hour darkness came over the whole land until the ninth hour. And at the ninth hour Jesus cried out in a loud voice, *'Eloi, Eloi lama sabachthani?'*—which means, 'My God, my God, why have you forsaken me?'"

Yes, Jesus most certainly understood absolute despair. Despair's darkness was so thick at the Cross that even the sun could not shine in Jesus' last hours.

What tugs at my heart here is the word *forsaken*. We will never know the anguish of someone whom God has forsaken because Deuteronomy 31:6 assures us that God "will never leave you nor forsake you." God allowed His Son to be forsaken to provide a way for us to escape despair. Have you felt despair's darkness?

✏ *Record your thoughts and write out Deuteronomy 31:6 in your journal.*

Francis Frangipane, author of *The Three Battlegrounds,* writes,

You will remember that the location where Jesus was crucified was called "Golgotha," which meant "place of the skull." If we will be effective in spiritual warfare, the first field of conflict where we must learn warfare is the battleground of the mind; i.e., the "place of the skull." For the territory of the uncrucified thought-life is the beachhead of satanic assault in our lives. To defeat the devil we must be renewed in the spirit of our minds![1]

Satan is in darkness. Wherever there is spiritual darkness, Satan is there. If we acknowledge that despair is darkness in the mind, then it's the mind where the battle will occur. Too many of us let despair's whispers of hopelessness and worthlessness become the truth by which we view our lives. Every good thing that comes then passes through this filter of despair's lies and becomes tainted and unable to unlock the joy God wants us to have and keep in our hearts.

Second Corinthians 10:5 says, "We demolish arguments and every pretension that sets itself up against the knowledge of God, and we take captive every thought to make it obedient to Christ." Christ says that you are holy and dearly loved. Christ has claimed you for His very own.

In John 15:9–10 we read, "As the Father has loved me, so have I loved you. Now remain in my love. If you obey my commands, you will remain in my love, just as I have obeyed my Father's commands and remain in his love." In the very next verse, Jesus takes the key and unlocks the chains despair has wrapped around your heart: "I have told you this so that my joy may be in you and that your joy may be complete."

✏ *Record this verse in your journal.*

Please know that I acknowledge there are times when this battle of the mind needs the accompaniment of trained Christian counselors. God is the Great Physician and certainly has ordained special people to administer specific treatments for people in need. It is not my intention to replace any help you are currently getting. My hope is that these principles will come alongside and assist what God has already brought your way.

JOY IS GOD'S REPLY

So once again we stand at the foot of the Cross. We learn from God's amazing sacrifice that because Jesus was forsaken for our sins, we never will be. If we know Jesus as our personal Savior, God will never turn His face away. God will never leave us. God will never forsake us! This is the foundation of God's joyous reply to Satan's despair. At the very core of discovering God's joy is the fact that God loved us enough to forsake His own Son so that we will never be separated from Him, His love, and His joy!

He will walk with us through every test, trial, tragedy, and triumph. He is there—wiping our tears, feeling our pain, holding our hands. And as hard as it is to understand, He is bringing good from our sorrow. God never wastes a hurt if we allow Him to redeem the painful circumstances of our lives.

✏ *Write in your journal about a time when God brought good from one of your past sorrows.*

"Those who sow in tears will reap with songs of joy. He who goes out weeping, carrying seed to sow, will return with songs of joy, carrying sheaves with him" (Psalm 126:5–6). The NIV *Life Application Study Bible* commentary says,

> God's ability to restore life is beyond our understanding. Forests burn down and are able to grow back. Broken bones heal. Even grief is not a permanent condition. Our tears can be seeds that will grow into a harvest of joy because God is able to bring good out of tragedy. When burdened by sorrow, know that your time of grief will end and that you will find joy. We must be patient as we wait. God's harvest of joy is coming.[2]

Is it really possible to be so filled with Jesus that despite the rise and fall of circumstances, we can actually have joy? Absolutely yes! In the book of Philippians, Paul outlined how we can have the unshakable joy that Christ purchased for us at the Cross. He wrote in Philippians 1:3–4, "I thank my God every time I remember you. In all my prayers for all of you, I always pray with joy."

Sounds like he was praying for his friends while he was off happily enjoying a tropical vacation, doesn't it? Well, Paul was writing from prison. That's right, a prison complete with chains, guards, bars, and less than adequate sleeping and eating provisions. Yet he was praying for his friends with joy.

Now I don't know about you, but if I were in prison, my letters to friends would read more like invitations to a pity party than a reminder that I was joyously praying for them. Yet, Paul's letter is filled with such words as *joy, rejoice, praise, hope,* and *faith.*

It is in Philippians 1:9–10 that we see the root of Paul's joy. "And this is my prayer: that your love may abound more and more in knowledge and depth of insight, so that you may be able to discern what is best and may be pure and blameless until the day of Christ."

If the battle against despair is in the mind, then it's no wonder Paul would use words such as *knowledge, insight,* and *discern.* He's telling us that the more we love God's Word and fill our minds with its wisdom, the more we'll be able to dispel the darkness with pure and blameless thoughts.

Verse 11 goes on to promise that in doing this we'll be "filled with the fruit of righteousness that comes through Jesus Christ— to the glory and praise of God." The fruit of righteousness is the fruit of the Spirit, which comes through a relationship with Jesus. Because we know Jesus, we can have joy unshakable, the kind of joy that brings praise and glory to our Father and draws others to Him. This is Paul's kind of joy.

Throughout Philippians Paul lays out principles that—if we choose to follow—will give us an amazing, despair-defeating joy.

Keep an Eternal Perspective: Philippians 1:12–30

Sometimes it's not the big, life-altering tragedies that knock our joy off balance. It's the culmination of lots of little joy-stealing moments. One Saturday my family and I set off for the circus. We were playing happy music, clapping our hands, and singing all in one accord. What a happy circus day! Then suddenly, my youngest gagged and sprayed the van with the contents of an upset stomach. Wait a minute . . . don't take away our fun family day at the circus!

Isn't that just like life sometimes? You plan a circus and it hands you a van full of yuck and a brokenhearted, sick child. What do you do when hopes and dreams are snatched away? The answer lies in seeing beyond the present.

Despite being in prison, Paul was able to keep an eternal perspective. Setting his sights on eternity, Paul wrote, "What has happened to me has really served to advance the gospel," (Philippians 1:12). Oh, if only I could remember to keep this attitude in my everyday life!

In verse 20 he went on to say, "I eagerly expect and hope that I will in no way be ashamed, but will have sufficient courage so that now as always Christ will be exalted in my body, whether by life or by death." Keeping your eyes on Jesus will give you the courage you need to choose to be joyful.

✏ *What are some ways to keep your focus on Jesus? Record how these can add to your day-to-day joy.*

Imitate Christ's Humility: Philippians 2:1–11

Nothing will kill your joy and that of those around you more quickly than having a critical spirit. Paul instructed in Philippians 2:1–2, "If you have any encouragement from being united with

Christ, if any comfort from his love, if any fellowship with the Spirit, if any tenderness and compassion, then make my joy complete by being like-minded, having the same love, being one in spirit and purpose."

Having the mind of Christ is no easy task. We may feel compelled to one-up others or to criticize, yet Christ always puts others first. We sometimes feel we must divide and conquer, yet Christ unifies with love. We are sometimes brash, but Christ is tender and compassionate.

To have joy, real joy, we must "do nothing out of selfish ambition or vain conceit, but in humility consider others better than [ourselves]" (Philippians 2:3). Christ came to serve. By following His humble example, we can discover real joy.

✏ *Make a list of ways you could humbly serve another. Commit this week to doing one of the things you listed and record how this brings you joy.*

Offer Yourself for God's Purpose: Philippians 2:12–18

We discover our purpose for being on this earth in the second chapter of Philippians:

So that you may become blameless and pure, children of God without fault in a crooked and depraved generation, in which you shine like stars in the universe as you hold out the word of life—in order that I may boast on the day of Christ that I did not run or labor for nothing. (Philippians 2:15–16)

We will shine with hope and joy as we apply God's word in our lives and offer to invest our light in others. When we are busy shining for God, it's hard to be overcome with darkness.

Have you ever asked yourself, *What is the point of everything I spend my days doing? Would anyone even notice if I weren't here?* I got to this point somewhere between three little ones in diapers and a struggling marriage. I knew God had placed desires in my heart to reach out to others and to fulfill His calling on my life, but despair kept tripping me up and discouraging me.

I kept hearing despair's voice telling me, "Look at you. Your life's a mess. God can't use you. You have nothing to give." Finally, I realized that no matter what stage of life I was in or circumstances I was facing, God could use me to fulfill His purpose. When I decided to offer what little I had to give, God multiplied my efforts, which brought rejuvenating joy to my weary heart. And I've discovered that to stay in touch with God every day and make myself ready to reach out for Him, I have to read the Bible every day.

The shining word of life is God's Word: God's amazingly powerful, transforming, and Satan-defeating Word. In his book *The Bondage Breaker,* Neil Anderson wrote, "You don't have to outshout him, or outmuscle him to be free of his influence. You just have to out-truth him. Believe, declare, and act upon the truth of God's word, and you will thwart Satan's strategy."[3]

That's why Psalm 119:105 says, "Your [God's] word is a lamp to my feet and a light for my path." It should go before us and direct the way in which we go. God's Word should be part of our every step so we can "out-truth" Satan and shine with joy for God. To do this most effectively we must know where our confidence comes from.

Put Confidence in God Alone: Philippians 3:1–11

God-confidence is a lot different from self-confidence. Self-confidence can leave us shaking in our boots when circumstances go beyond our ability to control them. Having God-confidence is wonderfully freeing, as we can rejoice that nothing is beyond God's abilities.

Paul had all the reasons in the world to be self-assured. His family, background, and experience were quite impressive. However, Paul wrote in Philippians 3:8, "I consider everything a loss compared to the surpassing greatness of knowing Christ Jesus my Lord, for whose sake I have lost all things."

Paul rejoiced in having nothing but his relationship with Jesus. Why? Because Jesus alone was his joy. Nothing, not even prison or death, could take his precious Savior away. And, because Jesus was with him always, he chose not to want, fear, or despair. Being this confident in his relationship with Jesus helped Paul to never give up.

✏ *What kind of confidence does Jesus give us? Journal your thoughts.*

Press on to the Goal: Philippians 3:12–16

If there is one area that keeps people from experiencing the joy of Christ, it is not being able to let go of the past and reach for the future. Paul assures us in Philippians 3:12 that though he is far from perfect, he has learned to do something very valuable. In verses 13–14 he wrote, "Brothers, I do not consider myself yet to have taken hold of it. But one thing I do: Forgetting what is behind and straining toward what is ahead, I press on toward the goal to win the prize for which God has called me heavenward in Christ Jesus."

For years I had no joy for my todays because of yesterday's despair. When I finally realized that holding on to my past was stealing my joy, I decided to follow Paul's example and let the past go. Not that I never thought of the events from my past, but rather that I chose not to dwell on them. I started looking for the simple things that brought me joy for today: a baby's laugh; warm sunlight on my face; a beautiful song; hearing someone say, "I love you"; memorizing an encouraging passage of Scripture. These simple things helped me press on for the joyful journey ahead and keep my mind's focus where it needed to be.

> *What holds you back from pressing on toward God's goal for you? Journal your thoughts. Also, list ten things that are blessings of joy in your life. Make a habit to add to and review your list.*

Keep Your Mind Steadfast: Philippians 4:4–9

As crazy as it may sound, I sometimes lose my joy over things that are not even true. Remember, the battleground is in our minds. To effectively dispel despair, we must learn to "take captive every thought to make it obedient to Christ" (2 Corinthians 10:5).

Paul gives us great guidelines for doing just that. He wrote in Philippians 4:8, "Finally, brothers, whatever is true, whatever is noble, whatever is right, whatever is pure, whatever is lovely, whatever is admirable—if anything is excellent or praiseworthy—think about such things."

It's crucial to be aware of what we are putting into our minds. Let us practice filling our minds with true things, not misperceived assumptions. We need to seek out that which is noble, right, pure, lovely, and admirable and study those things. Find the excellent and praiseworthy and soak it in. As we think on these things, the light of joy will dispel despair's darkness.

Know the Source of Your Strength: Philippians 4:10–13

Some days you will simply not have the strength to be joyful. I have had my share of those days where the old saying really holds true, "When it rains, it pours!" Paul encourages us: "I can do everything through him who gives me strength" (Philippians 4:13). God gives us strength to do not only those things that we want to do, but also those things we don't want to or can't do. How can God do this with our joy?

Our God is a joyous God. He can give us His supernatural joy, which is the best covering for despair. Nehemiah 8:10 says, "Do not grieve, for the joy of the LORD is your strength." The strength to choose the joyful path of life comes from God Himself. Ask Him for joy every day. Ask Him for amazing joy, joy that can't be explained or excused based on your circumstances. Ask Him for joy as a solid and steadfast foundation.

It is God's will for you to be joyful! First Thessalonians 5:16–18 says, "Be joyful always; pray continually; give thanks in all circumstances, for this is God's will for you in Christ Jesus."

✐ *Record this verse in your journal.*

The "be" here is an active verb that means we must actively pursue it. We must wake up each morning and ask God for it. We must go to bed each night thanking God for every bit of joy we've had that day. We must simply choose to find the joy in our *every* day! It is God's best for you to have joy and to have it abundantly.

A HEART RENEWED

My tears soaked Ashley's little blanket. I quickly adjusted the picture of the two of us taken only weeks before when she was still healthy. I told her to look at our picture and know that we could always be together in our hearts. My husband and I laid our hands on her fragile body and prayed.

Soon our time was up and the doctors took her away. I collapsed into my husband's arms and screamed in pain. He took me outside and with the wisdom of Solomon comforted me with his words. He asked me, "Whose child is Ashley?"

I told him she was our child. Gently, he cupped my face in his hands and told me that she was God's child whom He'd entrusted to us for just a little while. If He chose to take her, we had to trust Him and let Him.

There, outside that hospital, we released our precious daughter to God, and though I felt no happiness, joy started to resurface. I did not know whether this experience would end in celebration or sorrow, but either way, I chose to hold on to Jesus.

Years before, when my sister died, I ran from God. I could not understand how a loving God could let such a terrible thing happen. Letting go of God meant letting go of all that was joyful and running straight to the pit of despair.

I knew that I couldn't bear to walk those same roads of despair again. So I chose the higher ground, the path that Jesus marked out for me. It was a path lit with Scriptures, paved with trust, and marked out with signs of love. Though the exact route seemed unclear, its destination of joy was certain. This path would lead me straight to Jesus' arms of love.

When I walked back into the hospital, a nurse I'd never seen and never saw again, handed me a small white Bible. She told me it was for my daughter Ashley. "She is going to make it, and God wants her to have this Bible when she's a little older." As quickly as she had come, she was gone. I was stunned. I wanted to run after her and ask her if she knew something the doctors hadn't told me. Somehow, I knew I'd never find her.

John 16:22–23 says, "Now is your time of grief, but I will see you again and you will rejoice, and no one will take away your joy. In that day you will no longer ask me anything." The kind of joy that Jesus gives is unshakable even in the face of things we don't understand. I used to think that when I finally met Jesus face-to-face I would have a scroll full of questions that I'd unroll before Him. Now I realize that I'll no longer have questions. Only praises. Praises for whatever it took to bring me to stand before Him and share in my rightful heritage as a child of God.

Now as I watch my healthy little six-year-old run and jump and squeal and giggle, I thank God for every day I have with her.

I still miss my sister. Perhaps a part of me will always grieve for her, but God has restored and healed my heart. I have chosen to be thankful for the time we did have and to let go of the questions. When my family is together, we still laugh and we still rejoice. And in and among the joyous sounds of love, she is there.

DISCUSSION QUESTIONS

1. What is the difference between happiness and joy?

2. How could you fill your life with more of God's joy?

3. From all the "joy" verses we talked about in this chapter, which was your favorite and why? How did God speak directly to you through this verse?

4. What does it mean to "take captive every thought to make it obedient to Christ" (2 Corinthians 10:5)? What are some practical ways to do this?

5. What are some of the things that seem to steal your joy? How could you eliminate some of the joy-stealers in your life?

6. What are some of your greatest blessings that bring you joy?

CHAPTER THREE

FEAR IS SATAN'S DELIGHT
PEACE IS GOD'S REPLY

For I am the LORD, your God, who takes hold of your right hand
and says to you, Do not fear; I will help you.

.⦁.

ISAIAH 41:13

Genia was living a comfortable life. She had almost everything she'd ever dreamed of: a loving husband, a precious son, a newly adopted daughter, and a beautiful home. She loved the Lord and shared that love with many people whose lives she touched. Yet life had not always been picture perfect; Genia had seen her fair share of struggles and tragedy.

When she was a newlywed, Genia was diagnosed with cancer and underwent major surgery and treatment. She lost her beloved father to a sudden heart attack. She struggled with infertility. Twice she got pregnant and was overjoyed, only to have her dreams shattered when each pregnancy ended in miscarriage.

Despite these heartbreaks, Genia had made peace with the circumstances of her life and was even able to praise God for His work in and through her. Then one ordinary day, all of that changed, and her life has never been the same since.

In the course of treating Genia's home for termites, a mistake was made when the company drilled its treatment holes, and pesticide was poured through the ceiling onto the carpet in the basement. These toxic chemicals spread quickly through her home and triggered a severe chemical reaction in Genia. She became very ill. She and her family had to move out of their house in hopes that once the chemicals were purged, they could return. But no amount of cleaning was successful in remedying the problem. Genia and her family were never able to go back to their home.

Although her husband and children did not experience the same type of reaction Genia did, her symptoms were so severe she could not go into her house or even be around anything that was in the home at the time of the chemical exposure.

Every piece of clothing and furniture, the kids' favorite toys, precious family photos and mementos—all had to be put into storage and left behind. Eventually, all of these possessions would have to be sold, given away, or thrown out. In effect, Genia and her family lost everything. Every comfort of home was gone, disrupted, and uprooted.

The worst part was the severe health crisis Genia now faced. She was affected neurologically, which made it hard for this ordinarily bright, quick-thinking woman to concentrate, focus, and remember things from day to day. Guilt overwhelmed her because she lacked the energy to love and serve her family as before.

The peace her soul had enjoyed now seemed far away. Fear over losing everything, financial devastation, and crippling illness consumed her. She feared the impact on her children and her marriage. She feared the unknowns surrounding her medical condition. She feared every tomorrow, for it seemed each day brought with it more horrible circumstances. She constantly asked, *Why, God? Why?*

FEAR IS SATAN'S DELIGHT

Fear can be defined as the active feeling of losing control. In Genia's case she lost control of her home, finances, health, and even normal brain function. Think about your own fears. In each case, isn't it that you are afraid of losing control of something you hold dear?

I don't know what your fears are, but I can share with you some of my own struggles with fear. Probably my number one fear is losing one of my children. Every time I shop at Wal-Mart (which I frequent often), the first thing I see is a bulletin board filled with posters reporting missing children. I'm struck by how much the pictures look like my own kids—innocent, happy, and healthy. If it could happen to those families, it could happen to us.

You can hardly turn on the news without hearing of some tragedy involving a child. A child is killed in a car accident. A child is missing. A child eats something tainted at a restaurant and gets ill and dies. Just the other day I received a letter from a friend telling us that their youngest child had just been diagnosed with a fatal form of leukemia and that the doctors have given them little hope. In each case, the parents' ability to control their children's safety and well-being have been taken away. We love these little people and do everything in our power to keep them from harm, yet the possibility of losing them is real. That's frightening.

Another fear of mine is losing other loved ones. My husband, my parents, my siblings, my friends are all so close to my heart and so deeply rooted in my life. I know what it is like to have a loved one ripped from your life. The pain is deep and constant. But the possibility of losing another one is real, and that's frightening.

I also fear harm to myself. What if I were a rapist's next victim or cancer's next victim or some tragic accident's next victim? Not too long ago I was in a car accident that totaled my van. I pulled right out in front of a truck that I never saw. Based on the damage from the impact, I'm certain that if I'd pulled out only a second earlier, instead of taking off the entire front of my van, the impact would have been right at the driver's door. In an instant I could have been seriously injured or killed. What a wake-up call to realize that the possibility of something happening to me is real. And that's frightening.

Finally, I also have a host of other fears, some big and some small. What if my husband lost his job? What if I left the iron on this morning? What if my house burns down? What if I'm late getting the kids to school? What if my children need me while they're at school and I'm not there? What if my body gets fat, wrinkly, and saggy? What if, what if, what if . . . The worries go on and on, and at the root of every one of them is control—or rather, the lack thereof.

These fears haunt us and make us behave as though we don't trust God. Fear binds us and negatively affects our behavior, attitudes, and emotions. It causes us to sometimes stifle our children's independence. We're afraid of trying new things. God designed us to be creatures of adventure, and yet we feel paralyzed by our fears. We waste so much time worrying and expend so much energy feeling anxious.

✏ *Spend some time writing in your journal about some of your own fears.*

We all have fears, and Satan delights in each and every one of them. What twisted happiness it brings to his evil heart when one of God's children trembles for fear of losing control. For he knows that for us to fear losing control is a sign that he's got a foothold in our lives. It's like a crevice dividing each heart, a canyon where the waters of worry and anxiety flow. Sometimes these waters trickle along like a meandering creek, but at other times they rage like floodwaters through us.

I can almost hear Satan's horrific laugh as he taunts us and dances about, convincing us that we are losing control and must stop at nothing to regain it. He tricks us into thinking that worry and anxiety will somehow help. Yet in reality they add to the already rising waters in the canyons of our hearts.

Linda Dillow wrote,

> Perhaps the most striking characteristic of worry is its absolute impotence. Worry never changes a single thing except the worrier. History has no record of worrying warding off disaster. No tornado has been prevented, no drought averted, no plane kept from crashing, no child kept from falling off his bike, no teenager stopped from skipping classes or trying drugs. No heart attacks have ever been avoided through worry (though a great number have been caused by it). Worry is definitely counterproductive. Like the illustration of a rocking chair, it doesn't get us anywhere, but at least it gives us something to do, and women like to do something.[1]

We all like to feel as though we are in control. We think if we worry about something, maybe we can prevent it from happening. Remember the well-known acronym FEAR:

False

Evidences

Appearing

Real

Many of us are consumed with these flooding worries to the point of worrying about things that will likely never even happen.

Dr. Archibald Hart had this to say about the futility of worry:

Jesus was right. *In this world you will have trouble* (John 16:33). Some of us seem to have more than our share of it. But the truth is that useless worry drains away our energy for living and reduces our efficiency and effectiveness. We tend to worry most over things we have the least control over. The famous author-physician A. J. Cronin sorted out worry this way:

- Things that never happen—40 percent

- Things in the past that can't be changed by all the worry in the world—30 percent

- Health-related worries—12 percent

- Petty, miscellaneous worries—19 percent

- Real, legitimate worries—8 percent[2]

Satan delights most of all in deceiving us into thinking that we are in control. The more we assume we are in control, the less we depend on God. The fact is, God is in control. He always has been and He always will be. Satan knows this and hates it. He was thrown from heaven because he wanted to be in control, call the shots, make things happen, and overrule God. Since he knows he is not in control, it brings him great delight to deceive us into thinking we are.

✏ *Look over your list of fears in your journal. Will worrying about any of these things really prevent them from happening? Record who you know is in control over each of your fears. Examples: I fear that something will happen to one of my children—God is in control. I fear that my husband will lose his job—God is in control.*

PEACE IS GOD'S REPLY

The Bible does command us to fear one thing. Many times throughout Scripture we are told to fear God. "Now let the fear of the LORD be upon you" (2 Chronicles 19:7). "The fear of the LORD is pure" (Psalm 19:9). "Let all the earth fear the LORD" (Psalm 33:8). "Blessed are all who fear the LORD" (Psalm 128:1). "The fear of the LORD is the beginning of wisdom" (Proverbs 9:10). "Fear God and give him glory" (Revelation 14:7).

How can the fear of the Lord be blessed, the beginning of wisdom, and something that brings God glory? Simply put, because it proves we put our trust in nothing but God. We shift our useless attempts at absolute control over everything in our lives to residing peacefully in God's control.

Jesus knew we would struggle with control, fear, and worry so He commanded us to avoid it:

"Therefore I tell you, do not worry about your life, what you will eat or drink; or about your body, what you will wear. Is not life more important than food, and the body more important than clothes? Look at the birds of the air; they do not sow or reap or store away in barns, and yet your heavenly Father feeds them. Are you not much more valuable than they? Who of you by worrying can add a single hour to his life?

"And why do you worry about clothes? See how the lilies of the field grow. They do not labor or spin. Yet I tell you that not even Solomon in all his splendor was dressed like one of these. If that is how God clothes the grass of the field, which is here today and tomorrow is thrown into the fire, will he not much more clothe you, O you of little faith? So do not worry, saying 'What shall we eat?' or 'What shall we drink?' or 'What shall we wear?' For the pagans run after all these things, and your heavenly Father knows that you need them. But seek first his kingdom and his righteousness, and all these things will be given to you as well. Therefore

do not worry about tomorrow, for tomorrow will worry about itself. Each day has enough trouble of its own." (Matthew 6:25–34)

Certainly we are to prayerfully plan for tomorrow, but not worry or fear it. Linda Dillow writes, "It's easy to deceive ourselves into thinking, *I'm just concerned,* and gloss over the reality that worry is sin. Worry says, 'I don't trust God, I don't believe in His ability to handle my child, my marriage, my health, my job, or my loneliness.'"[3]

Oswald Chambers boldly writes, "It is not only wrong to worry, it is infidelity, because worrying means we do not think that God can look after the details of our lives, and it is never anything else that worries us."[4]

Dr. Archibald Hart tells us, "Anxiety is now the number one emotional problem of our day."[5]

✎ *Write each of these quotes in your journal and note your thoughts after each.*

To grasp God's peace and to see it stop the flood of worry and anxiety and fill in the canyon of fear in our hearts, we must trust everything dear to us to the God whose love for us is perfect. First John 4:18 says, "There is no fear in love. But perfect love drives out fear." There is nothing for us to fear for God's perfect love has conquered it all.

God has conquered Satan. God has conquered any evil that might come our way. God has conquered even death. It is all under His control.

So how do we transfer this head knowledge into putting our hearts and minds at peace? Isaiah 26:3 says, "You will keep in perfect peace him whose mind is steadfast, because he trusts in you." This is peace's sweet reply.

✐ *Record this verse in your journal. Also, record some of the prayers below and commit to pray these the next time fear sweeps over you.*

A fearful mind thinks, *Don't let anything bad happen to me.*

A steadfast mind prays, "God, I know in all things you work for the good of those who love you, who have been called according to your purpose" (Romans 8:28).

A fearful mind wonders, *What will happen to me in the future?*

A steadfast mind prays, "God, let me be still and know that you are God" (Psalm 46:10).

A fearful mind thinks, *What will people say about me? What will people do to me?*

A steadfast mind prays, "God, I will say with confidence that you are my helper; I will not be afraid. What can man do to me?" (Hebrews 13:6).

A fearful mind wonders, *What if something happens to my children?*

A steadfast mind prays, "Lord, I know by Your death you have destroyed death and You are the one who holds the power over death. My hope is in the eternity we have through You. Free me from my fear of death for both me and my children" (Hebrews 2:14–15).

A fearful mind thinks, *Fear is just a natural part of life. There is no way to escape it.*

A steadfast mind prays, "Lord help me to seek you, for you will answer and deliver me from all my fears" (Psalm 34:4).

A fearful mind thinks, *The world seems so dark and the future so uncertain.*

A steadfast mind prays, "Lord, you are my light and my salvation—whom shall I fear?" (Psalm 27:1).

Francis Frangipane wrote,

In the battles of life, your peace is actually a weapon. Indeed your confidence declares that you are not falling for the lies of the devil. You see, the first step toward having spiritual authority over the adversary is having peace in spite of our circumstances. When Jesus confronted the devil, He did not confront Satan with His emotions or in fear. Knowing that the devil was a liar, He simply refused to be influenced by any other voice than God's. His peace overwhelmed Satan; His authority then shattered the lie, which sent demons flying.[6]

Philippians 4:6–7 says, "Do not be anxious about anything, but in everything, by prayer and petition, with thanksgiving, present your requests to God. And the peace of God, which transcends all understanding, will guard your hearts and your minds in Christ Jesus."

This is where peace leans close and says, "I've given my reply, but now I want to share with you an amazing secret. You can have this peace, wonderful peace that can't be explained in human terms and that isn't dependent on your being happy with your circumstances. This peace will protect your heart from doubting and your mind from questioning. If you'll give me, through prayer and petition, everything you feel anxious about, big or little, with an attitude of thanksgiving, I'll give you peace."

Notice the words in Philippians 4:6: "By prayer and petition, with thanksgiving, present your requests to God." Let's apply what this verse is instructing us to do with our fears.

✏ *Think of all those things you fear. Ask God to reveal to you any that you've missed. Then write down what is the worst that can happen if this fear were to come true. Record these in your journal now.*

Facing your fears in this way will help you to relinquish their hold on you. We've already established the fact that worry and anxiety do nothing to change our circumstances, but facing our fears can help us realize that even if they come true, we will be all right.

For example, as I said before, one of my worst fears is losing one of my children. I can fret over this fear and go overboard trying to protect them, but still the reality exists that something could happen to them. If something terrible were to happen, I would be shaken to my very core with grief and pain. But I can face this fear by realizing that death does not mean the end since they know Jesus. I will be with them again, and in the meantime God will fill in the tremendous loss I feel with His love and compassion. I am thankful for whatever time God allows me to have with my children and am prayerful for them in the meantime. But I will not be held hostage by this fear.

I faced the realization of this fear when my sister died. Because she and I were eighteen years apart, in many ways I felt as though she were my child more than my sister. None of us in the family ever thought we'd laugh again after her death. Yet although we were devastated, we were not destroyed. God slowly replaced our overwhelming grief with peace. We will never forget Haley, for she will forever be in our hearts. Her memory does not reside in a painful place any longer, but rather lives in a place of peace and sweet remembrance. We are so thankful for the time we had with her and that we will see her again on the other side of eternity. We have found our laughter again and that, I'm sure, makes Haley very happy.

Remember to consider each of your fears in your journal with a prayerful heart full of thanksgiving for the blessings you've been given. Also consider each of these questions:

- What is the worst that can happen if they come true?

- Will any amount of fear, worry, or anxiety prevent these things from happening?

■ Are you at peace with the fact that God is in control and that He works everything for the good of those who love Him?

A HEART RENEWED

As you make your list in your journal and face the fears that haunt you, consider Job from the Bible. There are four passages in particular in the story of Job that have taught me much about fear. As we go through each of these, consider Job's peace and stead-fastness in his love and commitment to his Lord.

Job 3:25–26 says, "What I feared has come upon me; what I dreaded has happened to me. I have no peace, no quietness; I have no rest, but only turmoil." Job's first reaction is similar to what we would feel. Everything Job has ever feared—losing his children, his wealth, and eventually his health—has come about. His life is in turmoil, and he aches to the depth of his soul. His pain is so over-whelming that he can't even escape it through sleep. Can you relate to what he's feeling? Remember Genia from the beginning of this chapter? This is the place in which we last saw her.

Job's story continues with some friends giving very bad advice. Some of these friends feel that it is Job's fault that all this trouble is occurring. He must have some horrible secret sin in his life. His wife questions his commitment to the Lord, asking why he doesn't just curse the Lord and die. Somehow, through it all, Job holds fast to the Lord and, in Job 42:3, says, "Surely I spoke of things I did not understand, things too wonderful for me to know." And in verse 5: "My ears had heard of you but now my eyes have seen you."

Oh, how this Scripture captures my heart. I know what Job is talking about here, because whenever I've experienced deep anguish, I've experienced God in the same way as Job described. He had spoken of the God he knew and heard, but never had he personally seen God in such mysterious and breathtaking ways. Job's spiritual eyes had been opened, and He knew God as never before.

Genia also knows this deep revelation of God through pain. As I write these final words about her story, her circumstances are not much different than they were at the beginning. She still struggles with her health. The family is still struggling financially. Their belongings still sit in storage waiting to be disposed of in some manner. But Genia's perspective now is so much like Job's outlook in 42:3–5.

Genia told me, "I would not trade having everything like it was for anything if it meant giving up the sweetness I've found with the Lord. As a matter of fact, if things getting better means that I'll lose what I've found with the Lord, then I pray things never get better."

Amazing, isn't it? She realized some of her worst fears and now praises God for the increased depth of their relationship as a result. Doesn't this give hope to us all? Job and Genia are not much different from the rest of us. How encouraging to see what the human spirit is capable of and be reminded that this strength resides in us all.

Genia told me that two passages of Scripture have been a tremendous source of comfort for her. John 16:33, "These things I have spoken to you, so that in Me you may have peace. In the world you have tribulation, but take courage; I have overcome the world" (NASB), and 1 Chronicles 29:11–12:, "Yours, O LORD, is the greatness and the power and the glory and the majesty and the splendor, for everything in heaven and earth is yours. Yours, O LORD, is the kingdom; you are exalted as head over all" (NIV).

Genia says,

To me, John 16:33 is the pinnacle of comfort in a time of fear or tribulation. The fact that you do not just have to accept it or rely on someone else to resolve your troubles, but that you can be proactive and 'take courage' gives me great hope. Why? Because God has overcome the world. First Chronicles 29:11–12 puts it in a living-color perspective, one that lets me see God's complete provision in our lives. Both riches and honor come from God, and God rules over all. His hand is power and might, and it lies in His hand alone to make great and to strengthen everyone. These are two references that hit at the heart of where we are and where God has taken us in our journey.

I don't know the end of Genia's story, but I do know the end of Job's story, and it is remarkable. Job 42:10 tells us, "After Job had prayed for his friends, the LORD made him prosperous again and gave him twice as much as he had before." Job 42:17 wraps it up: "And so he died, old and full of years." Truly God is in control.

JUST PAST OUR FEARS
by Lysa TerKeurst

·ᛦ·

There is light in the rain despite its cold and stinging pain.
There is hope in the storm though it rages on like war.
There is life in each death even when we can't see it yet.
There is peace in our fear though His voice we barely hear.

You see, just past the rain the sun does shine.
Just past the storm a calm does lie.
And death isn't about the dying but He who calls us in the rising.
Yes, peace is ours for the taking. Just past our fears, God is waiting.

DISCUSSION QUESTIONS

1. What is at the root of our fears?

2. How do our fears undermine our faith?

3. How can the fear of the Lord be blessed, the beginning of wisdom, and something that brings God glory?

4. Review how a fearful mind thinks as opposed to how a steadfast mind prays.

5. Talk about some of the personal fears you listed in your journal and how the verses discussed in this chapter can help you overcome your fears.

6. How does overcoming our fears help strengthen our faith?

CHAPTER FOUR

DISCONTENTMENT IS SATAN'S DISTRACTION PATIENCE IS GOD'S REPLY

O LORD, by your hand save me from such men,
from men of this world whose reward is in this life.
You still the hunger of those you cherish; their sons have plenty,
and they store up wealth for their children.
And I—in righteousness I will see your face;
when I awake, I will be satisfied with seeing your likeness.

·❖·

PSALM 17:14–15

What a joyous occasion this should be, celebrating my thirty-fifth birthday, Jackie thought. *Some would call this the prime time of life. "Still young and vivacious, yet more mature and stable."* Tears welled up in her eyes.

Maybe for most this birthday would be a day of celebration and excitement but not for Jackie. She saw it as one more benchmark reminding her of the dream that was slowly fading. Like sand through her fingers, her hopes of getting married and having children were slipping away. Unable to comprehend God's timing, she resented every wedding invitation she received, every baby gift she bought for a friend, every comment from a well-meaning friend that Mr. Right would come along soon.

Her life seemed to be one Mr. Wrong after another. One was too negative; another seemed optimistic but was really just irresponsible. One was too pushy; another broke her heart. Another claimed to be a Christian but didn't want to go to church. One loved children—so much so that he'd had two with his first wife and two more with his second wife. The dating horror stories went on and on.

So, consumed with her feelings of loneliness, Jackie allowed Satan to lure her into a place of discontentment and distract her from seeing all the blessings from God that surrounded her.

❋　　❋　　❋　　❋　　❋

Janet sat on her bed and wept. Another negative test meant another month of counting, timing, waiting, worrying, pleading, and crying. Her arms ached for a baby to hold, and her heart longed for a baby to love. Why her? Why was it so hard for her to get pregnant, and why had God let her experience the tragedy of miscarriage the few times she had gotten pregnant?

So many questions had produced so many tears. Discontentment courted Janet daily. Not a day went by in which he did not show up on her doorstep. It used to be that patience would be with her some days and discontentment only occasionally. Now discontentment had captured her heart and consumed her every waking hour—and many of her sleeping moments too.

She feared letting go of discontentment. Letting go might mean that God would make her wait that much longer. Or worse yet, maybe He would never give her a child. No, discontentment would be her only beau. He wooed her and distracted her. He convinced her that God was not a good and loving God, so to exercise patience and trust in Him would be foolish.

❋　　❋　　❋　　❋　　❋

Patty's eyes longed to stay shut, but the scampering about of little feet and the baby's cry demanded her full attention. Another day was about to begin, though her yesterday seemed to never come to a close. The baby had been up half the night with an earache. Her body was sleep deprived, but her energetic toddler was ready for breakfast and activity.

There was a doctor to call, laundry to do, dishes to wash, and piles of papers that needed to be sorted and filed. There were socks to match and floors to sweep. There were toys to put away and pull out and then put away again. There were errands to run, food to cook, and then more dishes to wash.

There was a doctor's visit to make, and there were errands to run with children unwilling to cooperate. Patty felt overwhelmed and unable. She wanted help, but who could help her? Her husband's job kept him very busy and she had no family in town. Her friends all had lives of their own. They seemed to be able to handle all of this motherhood business, so why couldn't she?

Finally, while the kids were napping, she turned on the television, hoping to relax just a bit. Beautiful women with attentive, flower-toting husbands paraded across the screen. They had lunches in fancy restaurants and their nails done in salons. Nannies and housekeepers kept their homes tidy and picture-perfect.

Discontentment extended an invitation to resent her life. To resent the endless demands and thankless chores. To resent the sleepless nights and early mornings. To resent the smudges, crumbs, strewn toys, stains, whining, and crying. Resenting these things distracted her from God's precious patience. Patience would help her endure with a thankful heart, but discontentment screamed for things to be easier and less sacrificial.

DISCONTENTMENT IS SATAN'S DISTRACTION

Isn't it ironic that each of these women has something the others long for? One can sleep in, have lunch with her friends, and be responsible for only herself, but she longs for a husband. The one with a husband longs for children. The one with a husband and children longs for the kind of time the single life affords. Can you identify with any of these women? Are you distracted by some kind of longing today?

Discontentment is Satan's distraction meant to lure you away from the patience that is rightly yours when you accept Christ as Lord of your life. Can you hear him calling you? Calling you to resent where you are and distract you with things that could be. Don't mistake this for dreaming. I am all for having a vision for the future and goals to help you get there. No, this is different.

Discontentment is being unable to be at peace with where God has you now. It blinds you to all the good that surrounds you in your present situation. It keeps you from fulfilling the divine purpose God has for you now. It pulls the longings of your heart further and further from God rather than drawing you closer to Him. It steals the patience you need to wait on God's perfect timing and accept God's perfect will.

I know the feeling of confusion and longing. I've heard discontentment's call, and I'm sad to say that many times I've run to his camp rather than patiently waiting and trusting in God. I remember that when I was single, I was so distracted and consumed with finding a husband that I missed out on many opportunities for God to use me. I look back now at all the times I could have been serving and sharing God's love with others, but I selfishly pursued my wants, my needs, and my desires.

✏ *Record in your journal any places in your life where you feel discontentment's pull.*

Maybe your heart longs for a spouse, a child, financial security, friends, or a different job. All these things are good and desirable, so why is it that we sometimes have to wait for what seems like an unreasonable amount of time for them? Because God does not work in a human time frame. He works in eternity. He sees and understands everything from an eternal perspective.

Isaiah 55:8–9 says, "'For my thoughts are not your thoughts, neither are your ways my ways,' declares the LORD. 'As the heavens are higher than the earth, so are my ways higher than your ways and my thoughts than your thoughts.'"

Sometimes God's thoughts answer no to what you've asked of Him. There have been, and will be, those times when we never do get what we are asking for. In that case, acceptance is necessary to gain emotional peace. We are foolish to put God into a box for the here and now and try to make Him conform to our desires and our timetable. We must trust that He has our eternal best in mind and exercise patience to wait on His timing and accept His answer. We must also realize that whenever God says no to one thing, He says yes to something else that aligns with His good and perfect will. Oh, it is so easy to write those words but so hard to live them out in the middle of desperate wanting!

I remember as a teenager really wanting to go to a party after a school function. Some friends offered me a ride, but my parents refused to let me go. I was angry and felt they were being unreasonable. It wasn't until several months later when two girls from my high school were killed in a car accident that I realized why my parents sometimes said no.

God is our Father with the most tender care and compassion. We are His children whom He chose and dearly loves. Do you know this?

✏ *Record your thoughts in your journal.*

Ephesians 1:4–5 says, "In love he predestined us to be adopted as his sons through Jesus Christ, in accordance with his pleasure and will." Just as earthly parents must sometimes say no to protect and care for their children, so must our heavenly Father. And rest assured, just as earthly parents see and understand things their children don't, God uses His perspective, not ours, when making decisions and directing our steps. We must learn to rely on Him fully and follow Him with increasing desire for only His will.

Kay Arthur writes:

> If you are going to have an increasing hunger and thirst for God, then you must first get rid of the idols in your heart. An idol is anything that stands between you and God and keeps you from following Him fully. It is anything that usurps the rightful place of God so that God no longer has preeminence in your life. . . . Idols can also be television sets, houses, golf clubs, or careers. Idolatry can come in the form of a man, a woman, a child, a hope, a dream, or an ambition.[1]

It seems that one of America's ambitions these days is to win a million dollars. You can hardly turn around without hearing about *Who Wants to Be a Millionaire?* or the ultimate *Survivor*—who won, you guessed it, a million bucks. Now, I think that winning that much money could be good. Think of the ministries you could support, not to mention the incredible tithe you could give to your church. So, it stands to reason that winning $10 million dollars would be even greater. But if money is a gauge of the heart, then a survey showing what some Americans would do for $10 million dollars is disturbing:

7 percent would murder for the money.

4 percent would change their sex.

25 percent would abandon their family.

25 percent would abandon their church.

23 percent would become a prostitute for a week.

16 percent would leave their spouse.

3 percent would put up their children for adoption.[2]

This study revealed that two-thirds of the Americans polled would agree to do at least one of these things for $10 million dollars. What does this say about our heart condition?

"Now wait a minute," you declare. "I wasn't polled. I wouldn't do anything as horrible as that for $10 million dollars. Don't compare me with those people."

My friend, like you, I have given up much more for far less. We have all at one time or another refused to wait and have traded in God's best for what we reasoned to be good.

✏ *In your journal, record a time when you experienced this.*

Some of us have traded our sexual purity for what seemed to be one more chance at love. Some have traded the call God placed on their lives for more convenient or lucrative offers. Others have traded their relationship with God, their marriage, and time with their children for one more step up the corporate ladder. All in the name of discontentment, we hear Satan's call to get what we desire now, now, NOW!

Remember, Satan is crafty and forms cunning plans with our weaknesses in mind. What better way to paralyze our effectiveness for Christ than to make us ungrateful for what we do have and distracted by longings for all we do not have? This discontentment will eat away at your conscience and make you rationalize your way into getting what you want, despite God.

PATIENCE IS GOD'S REPLY

Our minds are reeling with distracting thoughts of discontentment. The words *Now, now, now,* seem to beat in our heads with every pulse of our hearts.

But there is another voice, a calmer voice. Patience is encouraging us to "live by the Spirit, and you will not gratify the desires of the sinful nature. For the sinful nature desires what is contrary to the Spirit, and the Spirit what is contrary to the sinful nature. They are in conflict with each other, so that you do not do what you want" (Galatians 5:16–17).

Then we hear the voice of patience again, only this time he's whispering. He's telling us a secret, a most important secret. "I know what it is to be in need, and I know what it is to have plenty. I have learned the secret of being content in any and every situation, whether well fed or hungry, whether living in plenty or in want" (Philippians 4:12).

Yes, yes, go on, you plead, your ears straining to hear this amazing truth. "I can do everything through him who gives me strength" (v. 13).

✒ *Record this wonderful promise in your journal.*

That's the secret. The same God who sent His Son to die in your place for love's sake gives you strength. The same God who gives unshakable joy gives you strength. The same God who gives unexplainable peace gives you strength. Now, in one amazing passage of Scripture, He explains how to be content, how to rest in the arms of patience, *for He will give you the strength.*

How? Well, at many stages of my life, I've had a hard time understanding how to be patient. I was constantly looking ahead rather than looking around. Looking around at all that God had purposed and entrusted me with at that time would have allowed me to make such an impact for Christ. You see, no matter what we have or don't have, God has given us *this day* in which to make a mark for eternity. Whether it is touching the heart of our eternal God or telling another of God's Son, there is a reason we have been given today.

Billy Graham says:

> It is Satan's purpose to steal the seed of truth from your heart by sending distracting thoughts. It should encourage you to know that the devil considers you a good enough Christian to use as a target. The difference between a Christian and a non-Christian is: though they both may have good and evil thoughts, Christ gives His followers strength to select right rather than wrong.[3]

The right choice is to wait on God and trust Him. Waiting can be an opportunity to discover God's best rather than settling for what might just seem humanly good. Waiting can ensure that we appreciate what we are given as a gift from God and not as something attained through human effort. Waiting can mean that God gets all the glory when the time finally comes for your prayers to be answered. Waiting can be the very tool God uses to make our patience grow. What are some things you are waiting for now?

✏ *Journal about the areas God may be using to grow your patience.*

If God says wait, then we will only know His best if we choose to obey Him. But waiting is not a passive activity. By all means, we are to actively seek God and all that He intends for us to discover during this waiting period.

To fully explore the incredible patience that is ours through God's Spirit that lives in us, we must take time to discover all that God has already given us. One day patience gave me a gentle prodding with one simple question, "Is this your greatest day ever?"

Let me encourage you to embrace this simple yet complex question, my friend. Let it seep down deep into your soul. Let your answer linger just long enough to change your perspective and settle into your heart.

The day God posed this question to me, I didn't understand why. *What a strange question to ask on such an ordinary day*, I thought as I hurried about my kitchen, packing lunches and fixing breakfast. I knew God was prompting me to answer this question He'd put on my heart, but I was on a tight schedule trying to get everyone ready and out the door.

I tied bows around pigtails and ponytails, kissed my husband good-bye, and changed the baby's diaper. I called a friend while I cleaned the kitchen and then called another while making the beds. Then the question stirred my soul once more, only this time it came with a slight twist:

If you had no children and then suddenly today you were blessed with toys to organize, bedtime stories to tell, and little messy hands to wipe, wouldn't it be your greatest day ever?

If you were paralyzed and then today you suddenly could climb the stairs, run after a toddler, jump up and down cheering for your teen, wouldn't this be your greatest day ever?

If you had no husband, and then today God gave you a man to do laundry for, help fold his collar over his tie, cook his favorite meal, and wrap your arms around as you fell asleep, wouldn't this be your greatest day ever?

If you had no home, then suddenly you were blessed with dishes to wash, beds to make, weeds to pull, and floors to sweep, wouldn't this be your greatest day ever?

If you had no friends and then today you had one who wanted your advice, another who wanted to come over and visit, and another who just wanted to share a funny story with you, wouldn't this be your greatest day ever?

If you had no sight, then suddenly today you were blessed with a blue sky to gaze up at, a child's smile to catch a glimpse of, and a beautiful flower to admire, wouldn't this be your greatest day ever?

If you had no Savior, then suddenly today you learned of the One who died in your place so that you could be forgiven, healed, and set free, wouldn't this be your greatest day ever?

I was brought to my knees with the realization that somewhere in the middle of all the gifts, I'd forgotten the Giver. Psalm 118:24 reminds us, "This is the day the LORD has made; let us rejoice and be glad in it."

I prayed, "Oh Lord, please forgive me for taking for granted the many blessings surrounding me. Please forgive me for spending time thinking about what I don't have, and sometimes grumbling about the responsibilities that come with all I do have. Thank You for this day that You have given me. So to answer your question, God . . . Yes, yes, indeed. This is my greatest day ever!"

✏ *Journal your responses to this question that so changed my perspective: Is this your greatest day ever?*

All patience has to do to break the hold that discontentment may have on us is to open our eyes to all that God has given us. To wait on God's timing is to trust Him and hand over control of our lives to Him. To trust God is to say, "God, You've shown me time and time again how very faithful You are, so even though I sometimes don't understand Your answers or Your timing, I will cling to Your patience."

Some people say, "Never look back." I say, "Don't forget to look back. We must look back." You see, when we look back over our lives we can see evidence of God's hand at work in our lives. We can trace a pattern of a Father's love and grace. We see His patience with us. We hear His call to follow His lead and trust Him.

A HEART RENEWED

With one amazing glimpse of God's truth, our entire perspective on life can change. Isn't it incredible that the power for change is available to us just by reading God's Word? His Word can break through even the toughest exterior. His Word can coat and heal even the rawest hurting spots. His Word can find its way into every crevice of our minds and hearts and draw us close to Him.

That's what happened with the three women from the beginning of this chapter. Though their names have been changed, their stories are real. Maybe you have even found yourself walking in their shoes. Well, there is encouragement in the way their hearts have been renewed.

Jackie's Story

Jackie got to the end of her efforts to make a relationship happen and decided to quit looking for a man to fill her needs. She realized that she could spend her whole life looking for something that might not ever come. So she decided to make peace with God's timing and His ultimate will for her life. If God said yes one day and brought her a man, then that would be a wonderful surprise. If God said no, then she would have no regrets because of all the opportunities she had being "single-hearted" for God.

Jackie said, "I decided to give up trying to do things my way and in my timing. I gave God my whole heart, and He brought me incredible opportunities that fulfilled me. The satisfaction that came from living in God's plan was so much more fulfilling than just finding a husband."

Though it was much later than her original plans, God did eventually bring Jackie an amazing husband. He loves the Lord and treats her like a princess. Jackie would be the first to tell you that God's timing was perfect. She is so very thankful that she did not settle for others who came along before God's best.

Janet's Story

Janet also finally gave God her whole heart and let go of her discontentment. Much like Jackie, she determined to continue to pray for a child and explore opportunities God placed before her through adoption. Though God's answer for Janet is still no, she has found such comfort and peace in trusting Him and serving others.

She has the most positive attitude and incredible heart for helping other people. She is the godmother for some precious children whom she loves as if they were her own. She works part-time for a Christian company, where she has many opportunities to share God's message of hope in the community.

A favorite Bible passage, and one she clings to often, is Proverbs 3:5–6, "Trust in the LORD with all your heart and lean not on your own understanding; in all your ways acknowledge him, and he will make your paths straight."

Janet says, "In human terms, our not having a child makes no sense, but in God's terms it makes perfect sense." The beauty of her patience to wait and trust God is that Janet realizes that her heart longs for fulfillment. In her mind, a straight path leads to the ending where her arms are filled with a child. But she trusts that if God's best path for her leaves her arms empty, God can still fulfill her heart.

Patty's Story

One day a friend of Patty's invited her to a morning Bible study. She really enjoyed all that the women shared and realized that she was not alone in her frustrations. Everyone had the same struggles she did. She had thought she was the only one and had let Satan heap guilt and condemnation on her.

What a relief to know that she was not alone. And how refreshing to hear godly advice about how to deal with her busy life demands. After several weeks of studying her Bible, and with encouragement from the other women, Patty turned off the afternoon soap operas and tuned in to the Word of God. What she gleaned from His truths changed her perspective.

She learned that patience lets us hear the "I love you" and "I need you" in a baby's cry. Patience helps us know what a privilege it is to hear someone call us Mommy. Patience reminds us to be thankful for little hands and feet, though they are messy and noisy at times. Patience calls us to take one day at a time with a heart of gratitude and discover all that God has to teach us through our kids today. Patience helps us remember how very patient God is with us, so that we can extend that same patience to our children.

Though there are those days when she finds herself slipping back into discontentment's blues, she is quick to recognize this as a call to dig into God's Word. He fills her, encourages her, and sustains her minute by minute, day by day.

DISCUSSION QUESTIONS

1. In Isaiah 55:8–9 God says, "For my thoughts are not your thoughts, neither are your ways my ways, declares the LORD. As the heavens are higher than the earth, so are my ways higher than your ways and my thoughts than your thoughts." How does this verse speak to your heart?

2. Comment on this statement: "Just as earthly parents see and understand things their children don't, God uses His perspective, not ours, when making decisions and directing our steps. We must learn to rely on Him fully and follow Him with increasing desire for only His will."

3. Why is discontentment such an issue in our society today?

4. Could you relate to any of the three women's stories from the beginning of this chapter? In what ways?

5. What was your favorite passage of Scripture from this chapter? How will this verse impact you personally?

6. What are some ways to protect your patience and prevent discontentment from creeping back in?

LONELINESS IS SATAN'S TRAP
KINDNESS IS GOD'S REPLY

Praise be to the God and Father of our Lord Jesus Christ,
the Father of compassion and the God of all comfort,
who comforts us in all our troubles, so that we can comfort those in any trouble
with the comfort we ourselves have received from God.

·❖·

2 CORINTHIANS 1:3–4

I'll never forget the day Beth and her husband told me they were expecting their first child. Their eyes shone with an excited hope and passion for all their future would hold. Then just a few short weeks later, Art and I found out we, too, were pregnant. Beth and I grew very close as we experienced the highs and lows of pregnancy together. Soon, we were the proud mothers of two beautiful little girls.

Beth and Steve seemed to have it all. They were leaders in our church. They had a successful business, a beautiful home, and now a growing family. A few years later, a bouncing baby boy was added to their family portrait, and it seemed as though nothing could go wrong for them.

However, tiny cracks in the foundation of Steve's life would soon cause it all to crumble. Steve decided it was no longer necessary to read and study his Bible. After all, he'd already read it through several times and knew all he needed to know. Spending time with his young family didn't seem quite as important as it once had. There were more business trips. Less talking with Beth about the future. More fights and more and more distance.

Then one day Steve shocked us all when he announced to Beth that he'd decided to move out. He needed space to sort through some things, he said. Beth was left at home with a three-year-old daughter, a six-week-old son, and a broken, bewildered heart.

What do you do with dreams for a future together when the "together" part no longer exists? Why did he leave? Beth wondered what she could have done differently. Maybe they could go to counseling. Was there any hope? All these questions ran through her mind and consumed her thoughts.

Soon we learned that there would be no future for their relationship; Steve had found a future with another woman. While Beth had been planning for their expanding family and their bright future together, he'd been seeing this other person in secret. His heart, once so devoted to the Lord and his family, was now cold and distant.

I know the painful details of Beth's story so well because I walked with her the early part of this unexpected turn in her path of life. I watched as she went through the motions of living while feeling dead inside. Life swirled around her in a confusing mix of new demands, new responsibilities, a new kind of aloneness, and new prayers. These prayers were full of questions from a heart full of hurt. Loneliness had stolen his way into Beth's home and heart.

LONELINESS IS SATAN'S TRAP

Why would a loving God let circumstances leave a person like Beth with the horrible ache of being alone? This deep ache comes from loneliness that leaves you without a shoulder to cry on or a person to cheer for you.

✏️ *Have you ever felt this sort of loneliness? Journal about your experience.*

Maybe because I am such a people-oriented person, or maybe because of the scars from my childhood abandonment, I long for companionship. I think most of us do. We need to know that we are not alone in facing struggles and celebrating victories. Life just seems sweeter when shared with others. But could we find that same sweet companionship with the One who ensures that we are never alone?

Sometimes when I'm studying or writing, God gives me one of those major "Aha!" moments, when I feel the Lord has just granted me a treasure of knowledge from Him. Usually my first reaction is to call and share this new insight with my husband or a friend. But God has shown me that although it may be wonderful to share this spiritual wisdom with others at some point, for now it's our special secret. These conversations are like whispers between best friends.

The Lord knows that these private conversations are precious in establishing closeness. He wants to build a solid foundation for your relationship so that when Satan tries to alienate you and make you feel completely alone, you can be certain of the One who sticks closer than a brother. It's been said, "You will never realize Jesus is all you need until He's all you have. And when He's all you have, you will come to understand that He really is all you need!"

John 12:46 says, "I have come into the world as a light, so that no one who believes in me should stay in darkness." Will there be dark and lonely times in our lives? Yes, most certainly yes. Because we live in a dark world, we will experience times of darkness. Times when we don't see God, times when we don't hear God, times when we don't understand what God is doing. During these times we have a choice to cling to Jesus' promises and seek His companionship or to walk in the darkness.

To walk in the darkness means to be trapped by our loneliness. Questions bombard us. *Why am I still single? Why isn't my husband able to communicate with me? Why am I so lonely even in my marriage? Why am I widowed? Why did God take my friend, my child, my parent?* Loneliness beckons us to walk away from the Conductor of life's symphony—to play our own song and get out from underneath the control of the One up front who's waving the baton.

✏ *Are some of these questions bombarding you now? Record these honestly in your journal.*

Loneliness deceives you into thinking the sad music the conductor handed you will be the only song you'll play for the rest of your life; that these somber measures will lumber across your composition forever. Loneliness tries to convince you that to walk away from God's perfect plan and timing is to write your own song, play your own tune, pick up the beat, and play the notes you want to hear.

Jesus felt the pull of loneliness. Jesus heard His closest friends say they would stand with Him no matter what—and then watched as one by one they abandoned Him. His eyes filled with tears as Peter, James, and John fell asleep when they were supposed to be falling on their knees for Him. His heart felt the pain of Peter's denials as His ears heard the rooster's crow. His cheek ached at the touch of Judas's kiss when His hands had only hours before washed the dust from this traitor's feet. Jesus knew what it was like to be utterly and completely alone.

✏ *Do you think Jesus understands your struggles with loneliness? Journal about your thoughts.*

Jesus felt the tug of wanting to escape what God was handing Him. You see, He would visit the horrors of hell before ascending to the holies of heaven. He would taste death's bitter defeat before finally having His cup overflow with life's greatest victory. His beaten and battered body would hang on the cross before He would be dressed in heaven's splendor and seated at the Father's right hand.

Jesus absolutely knew the pain of loneliness. Jesus told His three closest friends in the Garden of Gethsemane, "My soul is over-whelmed with sorrow to the point of death" (Matthew 26:38). Then going off alone, He fell on His face before the Father in prayer, begging for things to be done differently. Oh, how this Scripture captures my heart. God is wrestling with God here. This is the most pivotal moment in all of mankind's history. This is where God allowed us to peek inside the depths of His heart. This is where love for His perfect Son was called to make an unthinkable sacrifice for His fallen beloved. This is where Jesus' human pain collided with His divine mercy.

"My Father, if it is possible, may this cup be taken from me. Yet not as I will, but as you will" (Matthew 26:39). Have you ever begged God to change your circumstances? Could you say as Jesus did, "Yet not as I will, but as you will"?

✏ *Journal your thoughts.*

You see, for God to have taken the cup away would have meant that Jesus' loneliest time would have become suddenly filled with fellowship. Because there would be no danger, there would be no fear, and His friends would not have betrayed and abandoned and denied Him. Because Jesus would still be sinless and not have taken on the sins of the world, God would not have had to turn His face and forsake His son. God could have dried Jesus' tears and taken the cup from Him, and loneliness would have won. Yet,

Christ couldn't allow kindness to be denied its sacrificial reply. What had to be done at the Cross, Jesus had to do alone.

KINDNESS IS GOD'S REPLY

Jesus could have walked away and saved Himself, but He didn't. Why? For the same reason I couldn't leave the baby possums I found lying in the street one day. The stench of their dead mother was almost unbearable, but I could not leave those little creatures to fend for themselves in the middle of the road. They were groping about, crying and hissing, and something about their desperation gripped my heart. Though they were dirty and smelly, I couldn't leave them. Though it grossed me out to pull some from their dead mother's pouch and pick others from her pool of blood, I couldn't turn my back. Though it meant getting dirty and risking who knows what kinds of diseases, I had to help them. Compassion and kindness for the helpless compelled me and wouldn't let me turn my face and run away.

Jesus is the author of this compassion and kindness. He also couldn't walk away—because He saw you, as Max Lucado puts it, "right there in a middle of a world which isn't fair."

> He saw you cast into a river of life you didn't request. He saw you betrayed by those you love. He saw you with a body which gets sick and a heart that grows weak. He saw you in your own garden of gnarled trees and sleeping friends. He saw you staring into the pit of your own failures and the mouth of your own grave. He saw you in your own Garden of Gethsemane—and he didn't want you to be alone. . . . He would rather go to hell for you than to heaven without you.[1]

What an amazing act of kindness, and what an incredible example to follow. Many of us say we have nothing to give when dark and lonely times come our way, but Jesus taught us to look past loneliness into the richness of helping others.

We say we have nothing to give, and God says, "You're right, but I have something to give through you." Remember the encouragement given to us in 2 Corinthians 12:9: "My grace is sufficient for you, for my power is made perfect in weakness."

✏ *Record this verse in your journal and describe how it touches your heart.*

Maybe that is why the world hates weakness so much. If it is in our weakness that the power of God can flow most freely, then it's no wonder the world would want to cork up this power's flow. Everything about our society screams out against being weak, yet weakness resides in us all. No matter how beautiful, rich, powerful, and significant someone may seem, weakness is still there.

Behind the thin bodies and glamorous clothing of the rich and famous, weakness is there. Weakness knows no bounds. At every level of society, in every race, men and women alike have weaknesses. And be assured that along with weakness, loneliness calls their names. Sorrows and insecurities still haunt them. All the while God gently calls them to let Him make their weaknesses and loneliness count for something good. Many choose not to listen.

✏ *What will you choose? Record your thoughts in your journal.*

Jeremiah 9:23–24 says:

This is what the LORD says:
"Let not the wise man boast of his wisdom
or the strong man boast of his strength
or the rich man boast of his riches,
but let him who boasts boast about this:

that he understands and knows me,
that I am the LORD, who exercises kindness,
justice and righteousness on earth,
for in these I delight."

To walk the path that the Lord delights in, we must be willing to let God use the circumstances of our lives to reach out to others. Let's compare our hurts to stones littering our paths. We have a choice to do one of three things with these stones. We can use them to beat ourselves up, making our scars run deeper than they should. We can throw our stones at others, wounding them and making them also feel pain. Or we can use these stones to build bridges for others to walk across from their own darkness and pain into His healing light. This third option is seldom chosen, yet it's exactly what God delights in.

You see, to reach out with arms of kindness to another is to touch not only the heart of God but to touch the very body that was broken in your place. Jesus said, "Whatever you did for one of the least of these brothers of mine, you did for me," (Matthew 25:40). How many times in our troubles and feelings of loneliness have we stepped over Jesus and missed the miracles that come from helping others?

➭ *Journal your thoughts.*

In his book, *The Final Week of Jesus,* Max Lucado says:

When St. Francis of Assisi turned his back on wealth to seek God in simplicity, he stripped naked and walked out of the city. He soon encountered a leper on the side of the road. He passed him, then stopped and went back and embraced the diseased man. Francis then continued on his journey. After a few steps he turned to look again at the leper, but no one was there. For the rest of his life, he believed the leper was Jesus Christ.[2]

Let me ask you a question: Who was most ministered to, the leper or St. Francis of Assisi? It is at our point of helping others that we are most helped.

Brent Curtis and John Eldredge say in *The Sacred Romance,* "'Our creation is by love, in love and for love,' writes psychologist Gerald May. . . . we draw our identity from our impact on . . . others. . . . We long to know that we make a difference in the lives of others, to know that we matter."[3] Because God created us to love others, often He brings healing to us as we allow His healing to flow through us. When we refuse to extend this type of kindness to others, we experience a confused sense of longing.

Longing is wanting what you don't have—it is loneliness in its purest form. Often when we minister to someone else, our loneliness disappears. What do you long for? What are you sure would fill you and give you deep inner peace and security?

✎ *Journal your answers to these questions.*

I always thought getting married and having children would fill me, heal me, and give me the new identity I longed for. I have a wonderful family, but they can't fill me, heal me, or give me a new identity. For me to put that kind of pressure on them would be to suck the very life from them. They were not created to be redeemers; they were created to be receivers of my love.

I can honestly say my loneliest time ever was when I realized I had everything I ever thought would make me happy and feel significant, and I discovered it hadn't worked.

Recently I was speaking to a group of women in their early twenties. Some of their main concerns were centered in the fear that Jesus would return before they had the chance to get married and have children. I explained that having a husband or giving birth to a child is not really what their souls long for. Although being married and having children are great, these are not what will ultimately fulfill them. They are missing the fact that nothing this side of eternity can be all that our hearts desire.

Nancy Leigh DeMoss has written:

> Part of the purpose for those longings is to cause our hearts to become more detached from this earth and more attached to our true home in heaven. In addition, those longings help us to learn that true security cannot be found in people, things, or places. In fact to look to anyone other than Christ for fulfillment is to be insecure, because everything other than Him is subject to change or [being] taken away.[4]

Everything. Every loved one. Every despised one. Every beautifully decorated mansion, every pitiful shanty. Every beautiful sunrise, every breath-taking sunset, every devastating natural disaster. Every child ever born, every tear shed by the woman unable to conceive. It will all go away. With one blow of eternity's horn, Jesus will return and the race will be declared over. Every knee will bow, and in a single instant a sudden realization will come to every person that the thing the deepest parts of their souls have craved their whole lives is now there. In breathtaking, majestic splendor, Jesus is there.

No one will misunderstand this moment. No one will debate or doubt, but many will regret. What desperate sorrow many will feel that they never saw Him before. For He has been in and among us our whole lives. The One who could quench every thirst has asked you for a drink. The One who could satisfy your most gnawing hunger has asked you for a piece of bread. The One who could strengthen your weary legs has asked to be carried. The One who ministers to your deepest wounds has asked you for a tender touch. For the One who comes in heaven's splendor has worn the rags of earth. The One who descends on the clouds has walked in and among us.

The simplest way to say it is this: If you are lonely, reach out to another in kindness. For when we touch the one who needs healing, we touch the heart of the Healer Himself. And when He pours His healing through you to another, God's healing touches you first, and as a result you are healed.

> ✏ *Who could you reach out to in kindness today? List some people in your journal upon whom you want to bestow an act of kindness.*

In her book *Loneliness,* Elisabeth Elliot dedicates to Katherine Morgan the words she penned on the subject. They met in 1952 while working at a missionary magazine called *Voices.* She says of Katherine,

> I plied Katherine with questions about her life—her experiences as missionary, wife, mother, widow. She answered them always with good humor and often downright hilarity. . . . One day, in answer to a question, she said, 'I'm sure I'm a better woman because I'm a widow than I would have been otherwise.' . . . Her valley of Baca (weeping) has been made a place of springs for me and thousands of Colombians. For me she stands as irrefutable proof that to answer our loneliness is love—not finding someone to love us, but our surrender to the God who has always loved us with an everlasting love. Loving Him is then expressed in a happy and full-hearted pouring out of ourselves in love to others.[5]

What a beautiful picture of a woman who took what life handed her and allowed God to make it beautiful.

A HEART RENEWED

Beth is also an amazing example of what God can do with a heart surrendered to Him. After Steve left, Beth never thought she would feel love, happiness, or wholeness again. Loneliness gripped her and seemed to choke the life out of her. But one day she got down on her knees before the Lord and talked more honestly with Him than she ever had before. She told the Lord that day that she knew she was at a crossroads in life. She admitted to Him that she knew she could either walk away from His promises and truths and wallow in self-pity, or choose to walk with Him no matter where the journey might now lead.

She had been a Christian for many years, but never before had God called her to such a devastating place. Her walk with the Lord in days past had been uneventful and comfortable. But now, with so much change and turmoil, could she still follow Him? With tears in her eyes she said, "I choose You, Lord. No matter what, I am Yours."

After making the choice to let God work good from all the bad that surrounded her, she never felt that desperate again. She started writing in her journal, pouring her heart out to God every day. She copied out Scripture passage after Scripture passage in which God promised she would not be alone, that He held her future in His hands, that though she would weep for a time, morning would soon come. Day after day, page after page, Beth recorded God's encouragement to her.

Beth realized after a few months of writing in her journal that things were slowly getting better. She says, "In order for me to be able to move on, I had to understand that I was not alone. God had always and will always be with me. What hope it gave me to realize I would not always grieve. I would somehow come through."

Beth said she continually reviewed sections of her journal, looking for God's answers to her heartrending prayers. She repeatedly quoted her favorite Scriptures aloud and let His Word fill her mind and heart.

When Beth got involved in her church's singles ministry, she realized how many people were like her, hurting and alone. She dove into the ministry to get all she could from the teaching but soon felt God prompting her to give to others. Her focus changed from getting to giving, and soon her loneliness birthed new opportunities to pour Christ's kindness onto others.

Beth says, "We are each responsible for our personal relationship with God; therefore, through Christ we are whole and complete and acceptable. When you are single, you have a great opportunity to minister to others. I just decided to look at my situation as an incredible gift to be able to reach others whose situations I could really identify with. I assured them the pain does go away. The memory never leaves you, but the pain does."

In extending kindness to others, Beth felt the loneliness that once consumed her losing its grip. When I asked her what encouragement she could give to others facing loneliness, she gave me the following advice:

- No matter what, you have to be obedient to the Lord.
- Pray against bitterness.
- Pray for those who hurt you.
- Never give up hope.
- Find joy in the small things.
- Reach out to share God's love, kindness, and compassion with others.
- Keep a journal, and read it over to see how things do get better.
- It's OK to pray for things you want, but that can't become your focus. Your focus has to be the Lord and His perfect plan and timing.
- God is with you. He never leaves you. He hides you under His wing.

Beth is now so close to the Lord. He's called her to step out of every comfortable place she's ever known and walk hand in hand with Him on a new journey. Though it's not one that she would ever have planned on her own, it's one she would never trade. It is as Hosea 2:14–15 says, "Therefore I am now going to allure her; I will lead her into the desert and speak tenderly to her. There I will give her back her vineyards, and will make the Valley of Achor a door of hope."

DISCUSSION QUESTIONS

1. Can you identify with Beth? What most inspired you about her story?

2. What scares you most about being alone? How can Jesus ease the ache of loneliness?

3. Is it possible to be lonely even when you are surrounded by others? Share any personal story about loneliness you feel comfortable telling your group.

4. Comment on this statement: "We have a choice to do one of three things with these stones (that litter our paths). We can use them to beat ourselves up, making our scars run deeper than they should. We can throw our stones at others, wounding them and making them also feel pain. Or we can use stones to build bridges for others to walk across from their own darkness and pain into His healing light."

5. What does 2 Corinthians 12:9 mean when it says, "My grace is sufficient for you, for my power is made perfect in weakness"? How does this statement impact you personally?

6. How does it help dispel our loneliness to reach out to others in kindness? Discuss this statement: "If you are lonely, reach out to another in kindness. For when we touch the one who needs healing, we touch the heart of the Healer Himself. And when He pours His healing through you to another, God's healing touches you first, and as a result you are healed."

CHAPTER SIX

INSECURITY IS SATAN'S CONTROL
GOODNESS IS GOD'S REPLY

For God, who said, "Let light shine out of darkness,"
made his light shine in our hearts to give us
the light of the knowledge of the glory of God in the face of Christ.

·❖·

2 CORINTHIANS 4:6

Sharon Glassgow was born with a rare muscular defect. As she grew, the muscles on the right side of her neck pulled her head toward her shoulder and disfigured her facial features. Her right eye was drawn downward and her mouth pulled out of shape.

She tried to hide her disfigurement by covering it with her long blond hair, but the stares of others made her realize that hiding was useless. Her self-esteem was destroyed by the cruel and thoughtless jeers of her peers. Eventually, in an attempt to escape the harsh world around her, Sharon stopped speaking. Though she was in perfect mental health, Sharon was placed in a special education class and labeled retarded. Deep insecurities swirled and churned their way into her heart and mind.

Though I've never experienced this type of physical deformity, I have experienced the painful wounds inflicted by others that caused feelings of insecurity. There were the thoughtless comments from a dad who never knew how to love me, teasing comments about my out-of-style clothes and curly hair from my middle school peers, and comments from other moms that made me wonder about the way I parent my children.

What is wrong with me? Why did God make me this way? Does anyone really care about me, about my feelings?

Have there been times when these questions have jumped about in your mind? Have comments from others made you doubt your significance and wonder about your worth? Are there old tapes from bad past experiences that play over and over in your mind, stirring up feelings of insecurity? You scramble to hit the stop button, but all you can find is the one that pauses.

✏ *In your journal record some of your experiences with insecurity.*

INSECURITY IS SATAN'S CONTROL

Newspaper headlines reveal the tragic results of insecurity. A rash of school shootings have shaken America, and the common thread woven through these events is that the shooters were deeply insecure. Descriptions such as loner, quiet, small, picked on, bullied have been applied time and again to these kids who suddenly go on killing sprees. It's as if they decided that for one brief moment they would show all those who ever picked on them that they weren't so small after all. They believed guns would give them authority and that bloodshed would give them power over all who rendered them powerless. So the gruesome plans were made, triggers were pulled, and innocent people died.

Now, your own insecurities are not likely to lead to bloodshed. However, the pain of insecurity is real and is exactly what Satan uses to make people feel worthless.

Have you ever had one of those days when you just wanted

to crawl back into your bed, pull the covers over your head, and wish the world away? I know I have. Bringing up all my insecurities is the exact control Satan tries to use to render me totally ineffective as a servant of Christ, a wife, a mother, and a friend.

Have you ever felt these controlling cords tighten around you? Maybe you desire with all your heart to follow Jesus. Your legs ache to run to start a good work He's called you to do. Yet something, someone holds you back.

Being a woman in our culture can be especially tough at times. Satan attempts to control women with every insecurity imaginable. While you are standing in the grocery store checkout line, fifteen skinny supermodels smile up at you as you hold a bag of chips and your favorite ice cream. Suddenly you're bombarded with negative thoughts about your body, your willpower, your appearance. Before long, you've convinced yourself that you're a good-for-nothing slob. How much good are you in the mood to do now?

Or maybe you got really inspired to start a ministry at your church. You gave your time and put your heart into making it great. Yet, only a small crowd came to your first event and even fewer to the second gathering. Eventually, you convinced yourself that you must have misunderstood the Lord, and you stopped your ministry. Your mind reels with thoughts of failure, even spiritual doubts. Maybe you even get angry at the Lord for not making more people interested. You vow to never set yourself up for failure again. Who's in control now?

✆ Record in your journal an experience that came to mind as you read these scenarios.

Satan's use of insecurity to control a person's life is nothing new. Satan's influence caused Judas's self-absorption, which led to his betrayal of Christ and, ultimately, his suicide. But another disciple rejected Christ for a time and denied even knowing Him—Peter.

Our story starts in John 13:37–38. "Peter asked, 'Lord, why can't I follow you now? I will lay down my life for you.' Then Jesus answered, 'Will you really lay down your life for me? I tell you the truth, before the rooster crows, you will disown me three times!'" Jesus knew that Satan would soon wrap cords of insecurity around Peter's legs. Peter was eager to follow at all costs, yet he would be tripped and controlled by those cords.

Whatever the circumstance or situation, insecurity is quick to answer the doubter's call. Satan begins with today's doubts and failures and weaves in yesterday's insecurities to render his victim powerless. Yet all the while, a victorious and risen Savior calls us to remember His truths: God is, and was, and will forever be with us and for us.

He is Jehovah-Jireh, God my provider. God has provided Jesus to be our Living Water and our Bread of Life, able to quench the thirst and hunger of our souls. And He's promised to be our light. He provides a way out of the darkness of this world. "Arise, shine, for your light has come, and the glory of the LORD rises upon you" (Isaiah 60:1).

✐ *Record in your journal a time when you've personally experienced God as your provider.*

He is Jehovah-Rapha, God my healer. We know from Exodus 15:22–25 that God can make good from bad. Moses threw wood into the waters at Marah, as he was instructed by God to do, and the waters turned from bitter to sweet. What a beautiful example for what overflows from our hearts. We are told in Proverbs that the heart is the wellspring of life. God is the healer who will turn your bitter waters sweet.

✐ *Journal about a time when you've experienced the touch of God the healer.*

He is Jehovah-Shammah, God who is there. We are reassured in Hebrews 13:5, "Never will I leave you; never will I forsake you." In those times when you feel alone, abandoned, rejected, and, yes, insecure, God is right there with you. Never believe Satan's lie that God doesn't care. Rebuke his evil deceptions with God's Word. Rest assured that the God who records our every tear (Psalm 56:8) and knows the number of hairs on our heads (Matthew 10:30) understands and cares!

✎ *Write in your journal about a time when you've experienced the God who is always there.*

Jesus is calling to us with the truth of God. His truth can cut away the controlling cords of insecurity and free us to do the good for which God created us. Can you hear Him? Satan trembles at His voice. Listen, my friend. Listen.

GOODNESS IS GOD'S REPLY

Our ears are open and our hearts ready for the freedom Jesus' truth promises. Goodness replies during Jesus' last hours here on earth. When a person knows his time is coming to an end, only the most important words are spoken. Jesus shares from His heart the secret of fulfilling the call of goodness. Jesus says to His disciples in John 15:5, "I am the vine; you are the branches. If a man remains in me and I in him, he will bear much fruit; apart from me you can do nothing."

When a branch is attached to the vine, it is secure and able to produce good fruit. When a branch is apart from the vine, it is insecure and able to do no good thing. Therefore, the key to staying secure and able to exemplify goodness is to stay in a growing and thriving relationship with Jesus, who is your vine.

Watch Your Heart

Luke 6:43–45, Jesus says,

"No good tree bears bad fruit, nor does a bad tree bear good fruit. Each tree is recognized by its own fruit. People do not pick figs from thorn-bushes, or grapes from briers. The good man brings good things out of the good stored up in his heart, and the evil man brings evil things out of the evil stored up in his heart. For out of the overflow of his heart his mouth speaks."

Out of the overflow of our hearts we act and react. What is your first inclination when someone wrongs you or hurts you in some way? That initial reaction is a good way to check your heart condition.

John 18:10 records Peter's reaction when the soldiers and officials came to arrest Jesus: "Then Simon Peter, who had a sword, drew it and struck the high priest's servant, cutting off his right ear." This gives us a clue about the condition of Peter's heart.

Christ had just told his disciples, "I have told you these things, so that in me you may have peace. In this world you will have trouble. But take heart! I have overcome the world" (John 16:33). Instead of relying on the promise that Jesus had given, Peter decided to take matters into his own hands. He reacted in a violent, insecure way.

How many times do we rely on the promises of God to take care of us one minute and then take matters into our own hands the next? Because we are unable to control things, we become insecure and open to Satan's traps. God wants us to trust His goodness and concentrate on boldly doing good, for that is something we can control.

Titus 3:8 says, "I want you to stress these things, so that those who have trusted in God may be careful to devote themselves to doing what is good. These things are excellent and profitable for everyone."

Oh, how many times God has tested me on this point just to make sure I know it completely. A couple of years ago, I was asked to speak at a country club luncheon for several hundred women. Although I feel very comfortable speaking, I'm not exactly a country club girl. Oh, I've got the country part down just fine; it's the club part that intimidates me a bit.

Anyway, I spent some extra time in my closet that morning trying to find just the right outfit. I finally chose a light purple suit. That's when my great shoe dilemma started. After trying on several styles and colors, I chose a pair of bone-colored high heels. As I drove to the speaking engagement, I realized they were too small, because my feet really started to hurt. So, I decided to stop at the only store open at that time of the morning: Wal-Mart.

Imagine my excitement when I found a comfortable pair of white high heels on the clearance rack. I purchased the shoes and went to the speaking engagement. Everything seemed great until I walked into the country club and noticed that not one other person was wearing white shoes. These were the kind of women who did not wear white shoes in the wrong season.

I was so embarrassed. All I wanted to do was run away as fast as my little white shoes would carry me. But since running away was not an option, I decided to head to the bathroom and spray my hair really big. I figured if my hair was poofy enough, maybe no one would look at my shoes. Then I discovered that this country club provided spray in the bathroom. What a wonderful surprise. So I flipped my head over and sprayed and sprayed.

It wasn't until I flipped my head back over that I realized the convenient spray was actually deodorant. That's right, white deodorant. Panic started to set in as I realized I had no time to fix this mess I was in. Thank goodness Jesus spoke to my heart and reminded me Who was in control. So I brushed as much of the white out of my hair as I could and walked out of the bathroom and up to the podium.

I'm happy to report that Jesus brought good even out of this embarrassing situation. Many heard the gospel that day, not because I was strong and secure, but because Jesus was my stronghold and security.

> ✏️ *How do you think the condition of your heart affects your security? Do you trust that God is in control? Do you still trust that His plan is good even when bad things happen? Record your answers in your journal.*

True security is knowing that no matter what, you are accepted and loved by God, whose Spirit lives in your heart. When insecurities arise, check your heart and make sure you are listening only to the voice of truth. The Holy Spirit will lead you to good choices and good actions.

Watch Your Walk

After Jesus' arrest, Peter followed Him. John 18:15 says, "Simon Peter and another disciple were following Jesus." Peter started out walking the good path, following Jesus at all costs. Then good intentions were smacked by the serious reality of the situation. To be a follower of Christ meant danger. Peter again let insecurity control his actions, and in verse 17 we read of his first denial of Christ to the servant girl.

Every time I read this, I want to reach into the pages of my Bible and shake Peter. "Come on, Peter," I want to say. "She's just a servant. What harm could she possibly do to you? Don't deny your Master to her!" Then piercing memories of my own denials of Christ stop me dead in my tracks. All the times I could have told another person about Christ, could have stood up for what was biblical rather than what was popular, in the same way were denials. Could it be that the same old cords of insecurity Satan used to bind Peter were wrapped around me?

Verse 18 starts out, "It was cold." Yes, it was. Although the temperature may have been cool, Peter's denial certainly had the most chilling effect on the evening. Only hours earlier Peter had boldly exclaimed, "I will lay down my life for you" (John 13:37). Now he cowered by a fire among people who were likely mocking Jesus and looking forward to His demise. Where now was Peter's burning desire to follow, protect, even die for his Savior? Twice more, while Peter stood warming himself, he denied Christ. And then the rooster crowed.

Let's pause here to ponder a mystery in God's Word. Is it significant that the rooster's crow was the sign Christ used to call attention to Peter's denials? Think about when a rooster normally crows. A rooster crows and signifies that the sun is about to rise. If only Peter had realized that Christ's certain death at this point did not mean the end. Christ would defeat the cold darkness of this night and just like the sun, rise and yes, gloriously shine again.

I hardly think it coincidental that Peter was one of two disciples who actually witnessed the scene inside the empty tomb after Christ arose. Although Peter may not have understood the hope that the rooster's crow communicated, God certainly understood it for him. Peter saw himself as he was; God saw how he would be. Peter saw his sin-stained life; God saw one wholly forgiven and set free.

This is how God sees us as well. The next time you start believing that you are anything less than a daughter of the Most High King, holy and dearly loved, you must recognize the lie. We've covered this verse before, but we must say it again: Second Corinthians 10:5 tells us, "We demolish arguments and every pretension that sets itself up against the knowledge of God, and we take captive every thought to make it obedient to Christ."

Every thought that enters your mind should pass through a trap door that opens up if it's what Jesus says is true and slams shut on anything else.

Do you sometimes hear a voice that you think is your own saying, "You are a nobody and an ugly nobody at that. You're a terrible wife and your husband doesn't really love you. How could he love someone like you? And your poor children, no wonder they cry when you leave, make bad choices sometimes, and act the way they do. Look at who they have as a mother. Oh, and your friends. They may not say so, but they see you the same way you do, as worthless and disposable."

> *Record in your journal some of the false thoughts you sometimes have about yourself.*

Yuck. I hate that voice, and yet I buy into those lies, and before I know it, I am bound up in insecurity, able to do nothing and ready to quit everything. But Jesus instructs us to boldly take such thoughts and hold them up against who He says we are.

The truth is that God made you beautiful and special. "For you created my inmost being; you knit me together in my mother's womb. I praise you because I am fearfully and wonderfully made; your works are wonderful, I know that full well" (Psalm 139:13–14).

> *Record this verse in your journal and cross out all of your false thoughts.*

God will fill in the gaps where you are weak: "My grace is sufficient for you, for my power is made perfect in weakness" (2 Corinthians 12:9). "I can do everything through him who gives me strength" (Philippians 4:13).

God loves you. "For God so loved the world that he gave his

one and only Son, that whoever believes in him shall not perish but have eternal life" (John 3:16).

God chose you. Ephesians 1:11 says, "In him we were also chosen."

God's love for you can help you overcome anything:

> No, in all these things we are more than conquerors through him who loved us. For I am convinced that neither death nor life, neither angels nor demons, neither the present nor the future, nor any powers, neither height nor depth, nor anything else in all creation, will be able to separate us from the love of God that is in Christ Jesus our Lord. (Romans 8:37–39)

God has mercy on you when you mess up. Hebrews 4: 16 says, "Let us then approach the throne of grace with confidence, so that we may receive mercy and find grace to help us in our time of need."

God made you to do good. Ephesians 2:10 says, "For we are God's workmanship, created in Christ Jesus to do good works, which God prepared in advance for us to do."

To watch your walk means to hold fast to who Jesus says you are, keep pressing on, and do the divine assignments God has given—in His strength, not our own. Determine to live your life for an audience of only One.

Listen for God's Call

In John 21:3, Peter says, "I'm going out to fish," and the other disciples with him agreed to go as well. He was a fisherman until Jesus called him to be a disciple. This call was not supposed to be a temporary calling; yet with Christ's death, Peter did what many of us do when we start feeling insecure. He went back to the comfort of familiarity.

Peter had been called to take Christ's goodness to the ends of the earth, yet here we find him back in the fishing boat. And he was probably a very frustrated fisherman at that. Verse 3 goes on to say, "But that night they caught nothing." He was out of God's will and feeling the effects.

Then suddenly Jesus showed up on the shore, although they did not recognize Him at first. He told them to throw their nets on the right side of the boat, and when they did they caught so many fish they could not haul the net in. Finally, Peter recognized that it was His Lord, and he jumped into the water. He couldn't get to Christ fast enough. What a difference between Judas and Peter! And what a different outcome, as we shall soon see.

Verse 9 says, "When they landed, they saw a fire of burning coals there with fish on it, and some bread." Oh, how this must have captured Peter's heart. He had smelled a burning coal fire when he denied Christ. How precious of Christ to gently remind Peter of his denial, yet never belittle him with accusation and condemnation.

When they finished eating the meal Christ prepared for them, Jesus spoke directly to Peter. Verse 15 records Jesus asking, "Simon son of John, do you truly love me more than these?" Theologians differ on their opinion of what Jesus was referring to when he said "these." I think Jesus was pointing to the fish. Scriptures tell us the exact number of fish was 153, which means the disciples must have counted them. This was a huge catch, which translated into huge profits. Jesus wanted to know, "Do you love Me enough to finally leave your life of fishing, prosperous as it can be, and sacrificially serve Me in My eternally significant call on your life?"

Just as Peter denied Christ three times, Jesus asked Peter three times if he loved Him. The first two times the original Greek word for the love Christ referred to is *agape*, meaning pure, unconditional love. The last time Christ questioned Peter can be translated: "Are you even my friend?" Each time Peter answered with the word *phileo*, meaning brotherly love. Peter would have to grow some in order to love Christ with true *agape* love, and Jesus was patient with his response.

Jesus told Peter to fulfill his true calling—"feed the lambs," "take care of the sheep," and "feed the sheep." Peter answered this call in a truly amazing way. His insecurity was transformed into goodness as he boldly carried Christ's good news to thousands.

Peter's story ends differently from Judas' story because he was willing to run back to the Savior despite disappointing Christ. Jesus then instructed Peter to boldly go and share His goodness with others. Peter did as instructed and helped ignite the flame of Christianity throughout the world. But Judas gave up.

Two insecure men; two very different outcomes. Christ's goodness lived out through Peter's life made him great. The absence of Christ's goodness in Judas made failure certain.

✏ *Record your thoughts about Peter and Judas in your journal. How can you choose the path of Peter rather than Judas?*

Are you willing to turn from insecurity's control and run to the Savior? Are you willing to jump out of the boat of familiarity and trust God's truth about who you are? Goodness has given the sweet reply your heart longs for.

You've read instructions to watch your walk, watch your heart, and listen for God's call. Now do you hear the faint snips? Insecurity's cords, the lies that have bound and controlled you and your thoughts, are falling off one by one, Scripture by Scripture, thought by thought.

A HEART RENEWED

What encouragement we can gain from Peter through the Scriptures that document his transformation from an insecure and impulsive follower of Christ to a determined disciple ready to carry the good news, despite imminent danger, to all who would listen. The book of Acts records thousands coming to know Christ as Savior because of Peter's boldness and personal testimony.

More than sixty years after Christ's death, Peter wrote the book of the Bible that would come to be called 1 Peter. Three years later he wrote 2 Peter. Peter stood firm through years of persecution. He held fast to the Lord's call on his life. The same Peter who denied Christ now went boldly to tell the truth to all who would listen. Peter knew the truth firsthand—the truth that gives second chances, heals our hearts, and dispels our insecurities.

In 2 Peter 1:5–11, Peter wrote,

For this very reason, make every effort to add to your faith goodness; and to your goodness, knowledge; and to knowledge, self-control; and to self-control, perseverance; and to perseverance, godliness; and to godliness, brotherly kindness; and to brotherly kindness, love. For if you possess these qualities in increasing measure, they will keep you from being ineffective and unproductive in your knowledge of our Lord Jesus Christ. But if anyone does not have them, he is nearsighted and blind, and has forgotten that he has been cleansed from his past sins.

Therefore, my brothers, be all the more eager to make your calling and election sure. For if you do these things, you will never fall, and you will receive a rich welcome into the eternal kingdom of our Lord and Savior Jesus Christ.

Isn't it interesting that a man who was once held in such bondage by insecurity's lies tells us the first thing to add to our faith is goodness? When goodness replies, Satan loses the control insecurity's cords once afforded him. Peter calls us to posses these godly characteristics to keep us from being "ineffective and unproductive" in our knowledge of "our Lord Jesus Christ."

Our Lord. Personally, eternally, internally, and externally, He is ours. Given to save us but also to redeem us, heal us, fill us, strengthen us, and give each of us a brand new identity. No longer are you defined by the abuse and rejection you may have suffered. No longer is your identity wrapped up in past mistakes and bad choices. No, you have been transformed, grafted into a new, living, and fruit-producing vine.

Living proof that our God is a God of transformation can be seen in so many lives. We've seen it in Peter. What about the little girl, Sharon, of whom I told earlier?

Well, Sharon Glassgow's story is far from over. Desperate to help their daughter, her parents finally agreed to a risky procedure to help correct Sharon's disfigurement. Today she is a gorgeous mother of five with bright eyes and a beautiful smile. But even more stunning than her physical appearance is the beauty she has inside.

You see, during those dark and lonely years, Sharon and Jesus became best friends. He never saw anything but a beautiful young girl whose heart was totally devoted to Him. Though old feelings of insecurity still try to creep in at times, Sharon recognizes these thoughts as lies of the Enemy and keeps her eyes focused on her Master. He never saw her disfigured face because He was so enamored with the beauty in her heart.

Insecurity no longer controls and holds Sharon back from the call of goodness. She speaks to whomever will listen about all that Jesus has done in her life. Today she stands in podiums of churches around the country boldly proclaiming the truth that set her free. Sharon knows she is not who she thinks she is and she's not who others think she is. She is who God says she is, and that's wonderful.

What about you? The next time someone asks who you are, how will you answer? Oh, I know for social correctness you'll probably politely give your name and maybe where you're from. But inside, deep down where your body, soul, and spirit swirl together to form the true essence of you—who are you?

Jesus knows. He knows it all, and He thinks you're amazing. Incredibly miraculous. Worth saving. Worth forgiving. Worth healing. Worth dying for. That's why He stretched out His arms and said, "I love you this much."

DISCUSSION QUESTIONS

1. How does insecurity hold us back from a growing love relationship with Christ?

2. How does Satan use insecurity to control us?

3. Discuss this statement, "True security is to know that no matter what, you are accepted and loved by God." How has this concept impacted you personally?

4. What feeds the insecure thoughts we all have? How can we eliminate these?

5. What most touched your heart about Peter's story?

6. How can you apply in practical terms what you learned from Peter?

DOUBT IS SATAN'S WHISPER
FAITHFULNESS IS GOD'S REPLY

Therefore we do not lose heart. Though outwardly we are wasting away,
yet inwardly we are being renewed day by day.
For our light and momentary troubles
are achieving for us an eternal glory that far outweighs them all.
So we fix our eyes not on what is seen,
but on what is unseen. For what is seen is temporary,
but what is unseen is eternal.

•**∴**•

2 CORINTHIANS 4:16–18

In the middle of the night three people in official dress rang Stephanie Myers' doorbell. The doorbell graced a house that seemed to represent the ultimate American dream: a nice home, a nice car, and two nice children. Beyond the door, however, the charade gave way, revealing alcoholism and a cold distance between the hearts of a man and a woman.

Stephanie answered the door and wondered what could possibly have happened to warrant such a visit. Had her husband gotten arrested for driving while intoxicated? How horribly embarrassing that would be. After all, Stephanie had done such a good job of keeping up the façade of normality that few people knew about the downward spiral her husband had been on for over five months.

It wasn't until the visitors handed her a bag containing her husband's wallet and rings that the magnitude of the situation hit her. There, standing before her were a police officer, someone from the coroner's office, and a grief counselor. Grief was now an unwelcome visitor intruding on a life forever changed by one accident.

Her husband had been drinking and speeding, and when he hit the tree, he died instantly. Seeing the thirty-eight-year-old man who had been a part of her life for over ten years lying in a coffin was almost unbearable—unthinkable. Stephanie wondered what would become of her and her two small children.

Just yesterday she was a wife; now suddenly she was a widow. How could one second of time change the entire course of one's life so drastically? Where should she turn? Would she even survive? She prayed to God because she knew that's what you're supposed to do at such times. Although she was not a Christian, she believed God existed and that He had a plan. But she could not trust Him with every circumstance. She had no hope, no joy, and no eternal perspective.

Doubt's whispers were like lightning bolts cutting through a horrific storm. Stephanie longed for light in the darkness, but these bolts carried only deadly blows.

Could God really help her? Could He really be a Provider? Could He really be a Comforter? Could He really be a Safe Refuge in the middle of this storm? Satan would whisper, "No, no . . . God doesn't care about your situation. It's up to you to find enough inner strength to handle this. Don't trust God. After all, He allowed your husband to be taken and your life to be shattered." So many pieces, so many details, so much hurt—where could she possibly find the strength to face her worst nightmare?

DOUBT IS SATAN'S WHISPER

The other night, in sorrow and horror, I watched a network movie about Anne Frank, the delightful, whimsical child whose life came to an abrupt and terrible end in a Nazi concentration camp. As a young teen I had read the book that tells this story, *The Diary of Anne Frank,* but I never grasped the reality of what was going on in Anne Frank's life until I saw this movie.

Questions bombarded my mind: *What happened to the human conscience during that time? How could such evil run rampant? How could human beings treat fellow members of the race so barbarically?* The only reason I could think of was that evil had so hardened the hearts of the Nazis that they were incapable of seeing the truth of the situation. They did not see the Jews as human beings but rather as disposable and insignificant "problems."

That is exactly how Satan sees us—as mere pawns in a spiritual war. Satan hates God and anything that God loves. What better way to hurt God than to destroy the ones He loves the most? And Satan's tactics are not much different from those used in the Nazi concentration camps.

Satan strips a person of dignity and worth with his lies and distortions. He loves to see the gaunt appearance of a spiritually starved Christian. He charges his victims with the duty of digging their own graves of condemnation and worthlessness. He diminishes any chance of escape by surrounding his prey with the barbed wire of hopelessness. But as horrible as all of that is, the worst torture comes from his whispers of doubt—doubt that there is really a God who is in control and who loves and cares for His children.

Doubt makes people give up. It's like a child who sees a parent betray him—the one who was supposed to protect him from harm is *causing* him harm. Satan whispers, "Look around you at all that is bad. Are you sure there is a God? Even if there is, what makes you think He could ever love anyone like you? If God loves you, then why are bad things happening to you?"

✏ *Have you ever asked these questions? Have you ever wondered if God really cares about your situation? Journal your experience.*

Doubt says, "If God loves you, He'll only let good things happen to you." But inevitably bad things happen because we live in a fallen world characterized by disease, death, hurts, and troubles. But just because we experience troubles in this world does not mean that God has stopped caring for us. As a matter of fact, it could be the very thing that God uses to make us better, more mature people.

James 1:2–6 says:

Consider it pure joy, my brothers, whenever you face trials of many kinds, because you know that the testing of your faith developes perseverance. Perseverance must finish its work so that you may be mature and complete, not lacking anything. If any of you lacks wisdom, he should ask God, who gives generously to all without finding fault, and it will be given to him. But when he asks, he must believe and not doubt, because he who doubts is like a wave of the sea, blown and tossed by the wind.

Think of a lump of coal. He's happy being a little black lump because he has no idea that he can become something more. Then one day he's subjected to intense pressure. From every side he feels pressed in, uncomfortable, and cramped by his new circumstances. Can't you see how he could have doubts about what's happening to him? *Why me? Why all this pressure? Why all this darkness?*

What the lump of coal does not realize is that God didn't design him to stay a little black lump. God knew that with the right conditions and pressure applied, coal can turn into a rare and precious diamond. You, too, are a diamond in the making. Think how beautifully you'll be able to reflect the light of your Creator and how people will be attracted to your beauty!

How encouraging 2 Corinthians 3:16–18 is when it reminds us of this principle:

> But whenever anyone turns to the Lord, the veil is taken away. Now the Lord is the spirit, and where the Spirit of the Lord is, there is freedom. And we, who with unveiled faces all reflect the Lord's glory, are being transformed into his likeness with ever-increasing glory, which comes from the Lord, who is the Spirit.

What a gratifying goal to both reflect the glory of the Lord and become more like Him. The apostle Paul made this his life goal. Although he suffered incredible hardships, he continued to press on and give his life in service to the Lord. Paul had many reasons to listen to doubt's whispers, yet he remained faithful because he knew that God was working to bring something greater out of his hardships. In 2 Corinthians 4:8–9 he wrote, "We are hard pressed on every side, but not crushed; perplexed, but not in despair; persecuted, but not abandoned; struck down, but not destroyed."

God's faithfulness will not let you waste away as a lump of coal. Doubt would say, "A loving God would never let this happen," but faith would say, "God's love for you is the very reason it is happening." The key is to stay close to the Father and let Him carry you through hard, uncertain times. Stay close to the One who is faithful even when we are faithless. Draw near to the One who provides a way out of the darkness and a future of hope. Rely on the One who carries us when we are unable to find the strength to press on.

I saw such a beautiful picture of this principle illustrated during a news story about a father-and-son racing team. The boy, a quadriplegic, was unable to fulfill his dream of competing in a bicycle race. So the father had a special seat built on the front of his bike for his son, and together they competed in the race.

They competed in many races—even the highly challenging "Iron Man Triathlon." I was brought to tears as I saw this father running and swimming with his son attached, being pulled along using special equipment, and then once again riding on the front of his father's bike. The smile on the son's face was priceless. He could not have competed in the race alone. But through his father's strength he ran, he swam, he biked, and he finished strong.

How like our heavenly Father. "I can do everything through Him who gives me strength" (Philippians 4:13). So, why do we sometimes lose sight of this and start listening to the voice of doubt? It's when we choose to cut loose from the Father's strength and go our own way that we get into trouble.

Think about the father-son racing team for a minute. Imagine the son does not like the swimming part of the race where he has to get into water. Maybe the water is cold, or maybe the son doesn't like the other swimmers splashing, or maybe he is just afraid of water. The father tries to convince the son to trust him by reminding him of all the races they have been through together. Despite the father's faithfulness, the son listens to doubt's whispers and refuses to go with the father.

Now the son flails about on the shore, wondering why he's facing such struggle. He even curses the father for this hardship. Yet, the father stands close by waiting for the son to go with him. The son soon discovers that without the father, he is unable to continue and feels alone. Yet he demanded the separation. It's the son's choice to stay behind. But it's the father's desire for the son to join him and continue the race in the father's strength.

As a bystander, you can clearly see that the son should go with the father. We all know the wise choice for him—but do we know it in our own lives?

It is no surprise that Satan uses doubt to assault faith. To answer doubt's whispers with faithfulness means to be willing to accept all that God requires of us without knowing exactly what the end result will be. Faith requires you to take an uncertain step or sometimes even a leap into the unknown. But we do this every day, and we don't struggle with doubt.

Driving along, you have faith that other motorists are going to stop at red lights and go at green lights. You have faith that when you eat at a restaurant, the food is safe. A kid jumps off the side of the bed safely into his father's arms because he has faith that his dad will catch him.

In each of these examples there is an element of trust, because for most of us these things have proved themselves safe. Have you experienced that same, comfortable familiarity in your relationship with God?

✏ *Record your thoughts in your journal.*

The closer we are to God, the more we can trust Him. And when the voice of doubt calls to us and tries to woo us into questioning our faith, we can take uncertain steps knowing that faith has answered before and will always prove trustworthy.

FAITHFULNESS IS GOD'S REPLY

To understand how faithfulness replies, we must stand on the edge of doubt's divide. God our Father is holding His arms open wide, waiting for us to jump. Think of a little child jumping into his father's arms. The child probably would not so readily jump to a stranger. But he knows his father. His father has proved himself trustworthy and capable. The same is true in a relationship with God. If we will get to know His trustworthiness and capabilities personally, then we too will leap from doubt and land safely with an assured faith.

In deciding whether or not to trust the One with outstretched arms, we must discern what we are jumping from and what we are jumping into. We leap from uncertainty to the One who holds all of eternity in His hands. We leap from desperation to a blessed hope, knowing that God has our best interests at heart. We leap from questioning to trusting even when the answers are not clear, knowing that God knows best. We leap from listening to Satan's whispers to hearing God's faithful assurance that He catches us no matter what condition we are in when we jump.

No, this is not a physical jump. I'm not talking about being insane enough to go to the top of a physical mountaintop and throw the good sense God has given you out the window while throwing your body off a cliff. No, the leap I'm talking about is a spiritual leap from where you are now (falling prey to doubt's whispers) to where God wants your soul (abiding safely and faithfully in Him).

We leap and the Father catches. Two distinct acts. We must make the spiritual leap. The Father can't catch us and hold us until we leave the edge.

✎ *Do you feel like you are right on the edge spiritually? Are you willing to make the spiritual leap discussed here? Journal your thoughts.*

Throughout life's journey we will have to take many leaps of faith. The first one is accepting Jesus as Savior, but there will be many more. If accepting Jesus is the only leap you've ever taken, I challenge you to begin your adventure today. Don't stay where you are spiritually. Grow, stretch, and leap, my friend, *leap.*

I love the statement, "Neither go back in fear and misgiving to the past, nor in anxiety and forecasting to the future, but lie quiet under His hand, having no will but His."[1] You see, to walk away from the edge now without making this spiritual leap of faith would be to return to the fears of our pasts and the anxiety of an uncertain future and allow doubt to run rampant in our hearts. If we are to allow faith to grow and reign supreme in our lives, we must leave where we are now and thrust our souls into His hands. Then, and only then, can we "lie quiet under His hand" and know the secret of "having no will but His."

Lie Quiet Under His Hand

To lie quiet under His hand is to realize that we are but one scene in a much larger production. We may get so caught up in our own stories that we lose sight of the big picture. We lose sight of the Divine Director weaving and intertwining the lives of His beloved children. We lose sight of the inevitable happy ending that has already been revealed to us. We run about yelling, "Cut, cut . . . stop this scene, it is too painful. I won't play this part!"

Consider the psalmist's heartrending words in Psalm 77: "My soul refused to be comforted. I remembered you, O God, and I groaned. . . . I was too troubled to speak. . . . Has his promise failed for all time? Has God forgotten to be merciful?" (vv. 2–4, 8–9).

Oh, how the words from this psalm of Asaph match the feelings I've had when walking through life's dark times. I remember speaking similar words when the pain of my abortion held me hostage in grief and guilt. My feet would run to answer a baby's cry that I was sure I'd heard, and yet no baby was there. My mind was consumed with finding a baby that might have looked like mine. I would sit for hours in public places looking at other people's children, choking back the tears when I saw a child that had eyes like mine or hair like my husband's.

"Why didn't you stop me, God? Why didn't you make my car crash or make the doctor sick that day? Why won't you take this pain from me now? Have I sinned so horribly this time that your mercy can't find me?" Oh, how those words from Psalm 77 could have been written by my hand.

✏ *Can you identify with these questions? Record your experience.*

Then, in verses 11–14 of Psalm 77, we see that this soul made the choice to leap from where he was to where God is and rest in His hand.

I will remember the deeds of the LORD;
yes, I will remember your miracles of long ago.
I will meditate on all your works
and consider all your mighty deeds.

Your ways, O God, are holy.
What god is so great as our God?
You are the God who performs miracles;
you display your power among the peoples.

✏ *In your journal, copy out this incredible passage so full of hope and healing.*

Asaph cried to God for courage during a time of deep distress. The source of Asaph's distress was his doubt. He pleaded, "I cried out to God for help." But in verses 13–20, the "I" is gone. As Asaph expressed his requests to God, his focus changed from thinking of himself to worshiping God: "You are the God who performs miracles" (v. 14). Only after he put aside his doubts about God's holiness and care for him did he eliminate his distress. As we pray to God, He shifts our focus from ourselves to Him.[2]

When our focus is on Him rather than on ourselves, then and only then can we "lie quiet under His hand." Then we can stop asking God, "Why?" and rest in trusting everything to Him.

Elisabeth Elliot, wife of slain missionary Jim Elliot, shares an interesting perspective as one who has known her share of difficulty and tragedy. She says:

All of us may be tempted sometime to conclude that because God doesn't fix it He doesn't love us. There are many things that God does not fix precisely because He loves us. Instead of extracting us from the problem, He calls us. In our sorrow or loneliness or pain He calls, "This is a necessary part of the journey. Even if it is the roughest part, it is only a part, and it will not last the whole long way. Remember where I am leading you. Remember what you will find at the end—a home and a haven and a heaven."[3]

The Secret of Having No Will but His

Sometimes you question God's faithfulness because you feel He doesn't hear your heart's cry or because you fear His answer. Reading about a teenager dying in a car accident causes pain from the thought that it could be your child who is taken one day. A friend's husband has an affair, and again your heart seizes with thoughts of the possibility of an unfaithful spouse. You meet a woman who never married and sadly wonder if you will always be single too. You hear of a seemingly healthy person suddenly dying of a brain aneurysm, and thoughts of your own mortality grip you.

"Lord, protect my children from harm and my husband from temptation." "Lord, will you provide me with a mate?" "Lord, protect my body from danger and disease." These are all good prayers. Prayer is good, but we must be at peace with any answer God may give us.

This is where the secret of having no will but His comes into play. If we ask God to keep our children from harm, and harm still comes to our children, does that mean God is not faithful? Doubt's whispers would say, "See, I told you not to trust God. He doesn't care about you. You are a fool for putting your faith in God."

But to know God is to know that He is faithful. Faithfulness and God cannot be separated. So what do we do with feelings of doubt in the midst of a storm? We remember what Jesus did in Matthew 14:29–32.

> *"Come," [Jesus] said.*
> *Then Peter got down out of the boat, walked on the water and came toward Jesus. But when he saw the wind, he was afraid and, beginning to sink, cried out, "Lord, save me!"*
> *Immediately Jesus reached out his hand and caught him. "You of little faith," he said, "why did you doubt?"*
> *And when they climbed into the boat, the wind died down. Then those who were in the boat worshiped him, saying, "Truly you are the Son of God."*

Notice Jesus' response. It was immediate. Right away He reached out His hand. He did not stop the storm. He did not push the boat in Peter's direction. He did not throw him a life raft. No, those are human answers to Peter's problem. Jesus reached out His hand. Jesus wanted to touch Peter, to rescue him personally, and to stand with him in the storm and step into the boat together. Peter could never say it was a fluke of nature that the storm stopped and that this fluke was what saved him. Neither could he say that the boat saved him. No, Peter experienced the touch of the Master's hand personally and knew it was only Jesus who saved him. So should we.

✏ *How does this story encourage you in your own personal struggles and doubts? Record your thoughts in your journal.*

We, like Peter, should cry out to God. But could I challenge you to step back and change your heart's cry? Instead of crying, "Never let anything bad happen in my life," cry out, "God, when the storms come, will you grab me immediately so that I experience your touch personally and have more of your faithfulness in me?" Radical? Maybe. But if your heart's cry is always for more of God, then you will never fall prey to doubt's whispers again.

I am convinced that you cannot fall in love with the Lord unless you get to know Him intimately and personally. You can't quiver at His touch unless you know it is He who is touching you. Think about two people falling in love. They don't go from just meeting to being passionately in love in an instant. They long to spend time together. They long to touch each other and can't wait until the day when they can be totally and completely intimate.

God's Word compares our relationship with Jesus with that of a bridegroom and bride. Right now is your courtship with Him. The wedding is coming, but right now your main purpose for existence is for courtship with Jesus. For Him to woo you and for you to fall madly and passionately in love with Him and tell others about Him is the answer to the great big "Why?" of life.

Why must we face both tragedy and triumph? So that we can get to know intimate names for Him. He can't be our Healer unless He's healed us. He can't be our Comforter unless He's comforted us. He can't be the Great Lover of our souls unless He's touched each of us personally and has been allowed to love us intimately.

A few years ago, a storm was raging around me and I felt as though I were sinking. At first I prayed that God would stop the storm, but God did not. I kicked and screamed and pouted and begged. Finally, I went to God and cried, "If I have to continue to face this hardship, please at least help me to come out of it with more of You in my life." That day I penned these words:

MORE OF YOU, GOD

·❖·

In the morning when I wake,
When hard times come and my heart breaks,
Whatever your will, whatever it takes,
More of you, God, more of you.

In the evening when I am still,
Break my spirit, break my will.
Whatever is not of you, but in me still,
More of you, God, more of you.

In times of success when I shine,
Let me not say the glory is mine,
Let all praises be only thine,
More of you, God, more of you.

In times of sadness when I'm down,
May my spirit still smile, never frown.
My hope in you the eternity I've found,
More of you, God, more of you.

Then, when I live my last day,
I have one thing I hope you'll say,
"You did well, my child, when you prayed,
More of you, God, more of you."

That's the secret of having no will but His. That's why the apostle Paul was able to say, "For to me, to live is Christ and to die is gain" (Philippians 1:21). To live meant to continue his mission on earth, and that was good. To die meant being face-to-face with the Great Lover of his soul, Jesus, and that would be great. To live or to die pretty much covered the spectrum, and in each case he was fine. He had no will but God's will. Trusting God in this way is difficult but life changing.

"The ultimate source of human woundedness comes from dislocations of not making God the center of our lives. Having put ourselves out of joint with God, we have wounded ourselves."⁴ We sell our relationship with the Lord short if we just look at Him as our helper to get through one more day or our fire insurance for eternity. It's about so much more than that. I suppose this brings us to faithfulness' ultimate response: Are we willing to make God the center of every part of our lives? Are we willing to trust Him to hold everything in His hands and give and take as He knows best? After all, would our doubt change the outcome of anything anyhow?

✍ *Journal your answers to these questions.*

Doubt does nothing but pull us from the edge of hope where our Father waits to catch His beloved child. Doubt's whispers are lies from the lips of one who is destined to be "thrown into the lake of burning sulfur" (Revelation 20:10). Satan's whispers say that faith is for fools and cause us to lose heart. Yet Satan himself is the ultimate fool and is only looking for other faithless fools to join him. Remember the old saying, "Misery loves company."

Hebrews 11:1 says, "Faith is being sure of what we hope for and certain of what we do not see." Faith gives his full, resounding reply to doubt before the Father ever catches the one who leaps. You see, faith is founded on trust that the Father will catch you safely. Your faith is victorious in defeating doubt the second your feet leave the edge. And rest assured, we don't jump to prove God is faithful. God has already proved that. We jump to experience His faithfulness personally.

We jump. He catches. Then He whispers, "You are my beloved, my faithful daughter. Now let's venture from this mountain top to another and then another. I have such heights I want to show you and such depths of your soul to reveal." Then hand in hand you journey on together.

A HEART RENEWED

Along our journey of life we all have felt the tug of unmet expectations and disappointments. Sometimes they are as small as getting the wrong food at the drive-through window, and other times as huge as losing someone we love. In any case, nothing of this world can ever meet or fulfill the deepest longing of our souls. Not the most yummy food or a wonderful relationship with another person. Those things will always fade, always die, always leave gaps. Only an intimate relationship with Jesus can ease the constant ache in our souls.

Stephanie always thought that getting married and establishing the "perfect life" would make her feel complete. But when she had all of that, the ache was still there. The ache grew more and more painful as her perfect life started to crumble. Piece by piece, bit by bit, things were falling apart. In the funeral home, with her husband gone, she realized life as she had known it was over. No more charades. No more pretending. Doubt's whispers overwhelmed her.

A year later she tried to fill in the gaps in her heart with another man, but things fell apart once again. Broken and alone, she finally heard the call of her Savior. He had been calling for a long time, but she had been too consumed with figuring everything out for herself to hear Him. For the first time, she answered His call and told Him yes. Yes she would trust Him, not as a remote God but as a personal and intimate Savior.

Stephanie now says, "If you don't put the Lord first, you will never have the peace and joy your heart longs for because anything else always leaves gaps—whether it's money, people, drugs, alcohol, or anything else the world has to offer."

She now looks at her life very differently. Doubt no longer consumes her. Her faith is growing and thriving. She brought tears to my eyes when she told me, "God's given me this opportunity to be as close to Him as I have ever been. What a gift! Seeing my circumstances as a blessing rather than a curse has changed my whole perspective."

Stephanie reached for Jesus' hand and at first cried out like Peter, "Save me!" But the Master didn't touch Stephanie just once; He reached for her constantly, and the more she took His hand, the more her faith grew. Now her heart's cry is not, "Save me!" but "Grow me!"

Recently she told me that God was leading her to sell her house and move to another state. She put her house up for sale, and for months now has gone through the stress of having her home on the market. She could question God's timing and get angry at the inconvenience and uncertainty of her situation, but that isn't what she's doing. She's walking step-by-step, day by day, hand in hand with our perfect and eternal God. She's trusting and believing and thanking God for evidences of His hand at work in her and through her situation.

Her heart's cry in both the big and the small is now, "More of you, God, more of you!"

DISCUSSION QUESTIONS

1. Have you ever felt like the little lump of coal described in this chapter? What did you learn through your experience?

2. How was Paul able to press on despite incredible hardships? What encouragement does he offer us?

3. Discuss this statement: "To lie quiet under His hand is to realize that we are but one scene in a much larger production. Many of us get so caught up in our own stories that we lose sight of the big picture."

4. What does it mean to take a spiritual leap from doubt to faith? If you have a personal example feel free to share it.

5. What is the "secret of having no will but His?" How does this impact you personally?

6. Hebrews 11:1 says, "Now faith is being sure of what we hope for and certain of what we do not see." Discuss the meaning of this verse as it relates to the poem "More of You, God," which appears near the end of this chapter.

BITTERNESS IS SATAN'S REVENGE GENTLENESS IS GOD'S REPLY

Therefore, as God's chosen people, holy and dearly loved,
clothe yourselves with compassion, kindness,
humility, gentleness and patience.
Bear with each other and forgive whatever grievances
you may have against one another.
Forgive as the Lord forgave you.

·❖·

COLOSSIANS 3:12–13

There are certain tragic moments that are forever etched in my mind. I vividly remember seeing Princess Diana's wedding and then, years later, her untimely death and funeral. I remember seeing the news clip about the Space Shuttle Challenger when it exploded shortly after takeoff, killing all those aboard. I remember when our nation went to war for the first time in my lifetime. But the historic moments that haunt me and that have probably done more to both horrify and wake up our nation are the flood of school shootings we've witnessed in the past few years.

High schools are supposed to be places where bright futures are birthed and nurtured. Instead, in the hands of angry killers, some have become places of horror and death. Such was the case on April 20, 1999, when two troubled teens stormed Columbine High School in Littleton, Colorado, killing one teacher and twelve students and wounding many others. One of those killed was Rachel Scott. Though I never knew her personally, her life and her parents' response to her death have truly inspired me.

Rachel's story especially moved me because she had many of the same interests and passions I did as a teen. She loved to perform on stage. She loved to write poetry. She loved to reach out to others and show compassion to people others shunned. She loved her youth group, and she loved the Lord. Although we were alike in these ways, one difference was clear. Rachel had reached a level of spiritual maturity in seventeen years that has taken me nearly twice as many years to reach. This is what made her truly remarkable and makes her story so inspiring. Not that she was perfect—she had her flaws and struggles, as we all do—but she desired to be totally surrendered to God.

In their book *Rachel's Tears: The Spiritual Journey of the Columbine Martyr Rachel Scott,* Rachel's parents, Beth Nimmo and Darrell Scott, recount her final moments in the hands of merciless killers. Rachel was having lunch outside the Columbine library with her friend Richard Castaldo when Eric Harris and Dylan Klebold began shooting at them, severing Richard's spine and wounding Rachel twice in her legs and once in her torso.

> As Richard lay stunned and Rachel attempted to crawl to safety, the shooters began to walk away, only to return seconds later. At that point, Harris reportedly grabbed Rachel by her hair, held her head up, an asked her the question: "Do you believe in God?"
> "You know I do," replied Rachel.
> "Then go be with Him," responded Harris before shooting her in the head.[1]

And then she was gone. In one brief moment, her family's lives were changed forever, as were Rachel's friends, the other students of Columbine, the Littleton community, the nation, and the world. How, as a parent, do you deal with such horror? How do you *not* accept Satan's invitation to bitter revenge?

BITTERNESS IS SATAN'S REVENGE

Bitterness loves to blow his seeds through a person's thoughts. Seeking to take over the rich soil of a human heart, these seeds convince a person that growing them will produce many flowers—one of which is the weed of sweet revenge. Yet though revenge may seem sweet, this weed's roots are nothing but bitter. Once this bitter root claims a place in your heart, it will produce more weeds, *stubborn* weeds, the kind that spread and continue to grow until the very last tentacle of the root is pulled up and destroyed.

Have you ever had a weed pop up in your yard, only to pull the stem and the flower off, pleased that you've rid yourself of the problem? "Ah," you say. "Now my yard is nice and soft . . . gentle to the foot and pleasing to the eye." But before you know it, the weed is back—and now he's brought friends with him.

You've got a whole weed fiesta in your front yard. Frantically you run about yanking their stems and flowers and stomping them into the sidewalk. A little sweaty from all this work, you flex your muscles and give a Rambolike glance at the smashed weeds. *No weed will get the best of me,* you think, smirking.

Then a light rain shower and a few good days of sunshine provide just the right conditions for . . . not just a *gathering* of weed friends, but a whole *community* residing in your front yard. Where are they coming from? Why do they seem to be gone one day and back with a vengeance a few days later? You lament and toil over your weed problem.

Finally, someone shares the secret of weed control and prevention with you: You've got to get weeds at the roots to kill them. Just pulling the flowers and stems off will not kill them. To make sure the weed is dead, really dead, never-coming-back dead, you must eliminate the root of the weed.

How alike are the garden and the human heart. You see, we too have weeds that have been planted and cultivated in our hearts. Hebrews 12:15 says, "See to it that no one misses the grace of God and that no bitter root grows up to cause trouble and defile many." The root of bitterness will produce a whole crop of weeds such as Ephesians 4:31 instructs us to rid ourselves of: "rage and anger, brawling and slander, along with every form of malice."

For years, I did not understand that bitterness had a hold on my heart. Although I was unaware of the bitter roots, I was well aware of the weeds those roots produced. I was filled with rage and anger. Bitterness so filled my heart's garden that the beautiful fruit of the Spirit was choked out.

The bitter roots growing in my heart had a strong, extensive root system. They had been watered and fertilized over the years because of my poor relationship with my biological father. I could not understand why my dad did not love me. I could not understand why he'd want to hurt me. For years, I sought to fill the emptiness left by my father with other men, but time and time again I wound up hurt.

If only my dad had loved me, I wouldn't have struggled with being so insecure. If only my dad had loved me, I wouldn't have looked for love in all the wrong places. If only my dad had loved me, I wouldn't have sought intimacy through premarital sex. If only my dad had loved me, I wouldn't have wound up in that abortion clinic. If only . . . If only . . . If only . . .

I had experienced so much hurt and so much pain. So I bought Satan's lies and planted seeds of bitterness that harvested a mighty crop of weeds. How could I be anything but bitter? It was my right. It was my only revenge.

GENTLENESS IS GOD'S REPLY

When I became a mother, I vowed to love my children the way

I'd always wanted my dad to love me. I made all kinds of promises to myself about the things I would and would not do. However, the harder I tried, the more I realized that those promises were hard to keep. Actually, those promises were *impossible* to keep.

In my mind, I saw what kind of mother and wife I wanted to be, but the reality of how I treated my family was very different from my desires. I found myself yelling at my kids and becoming infuriated with my husband. I was filled with anger, rage, and all of the other weeds that bitterness is so famous for growing. Something had to change. Someone had to change. And I knew that someone was me.

Finally, I realized through reading God's Word that I could not give my husband and my children a heart of love, joy, peace, patience, kindness, goodness, faithfulness, gentleness, and self-control until I killed the weeds that were choking the life out of my spirit.

Finally, gentleness answered my heart's cry. He is waiting to answer yours as well. I realized that I could never become the person Christ wanted me to be until I let go of my bitterness and forgave the people who had hurt me.

✏ *Have you struggled in this same way with some of your relationships, past or present? Record your thoughts and feelings in your journal.*

Ask God to Search You and Test You

As we scan the horizon of our hearts looking for weeds that give evidence of bitter roots, we must ask God to reveal them to us. We must be willing to follow Psalm 139:23–24 and pray, "Search me, O God, and know my heart; test me and know my anxious thoughts. See if there is any offensive way in me, and lead me in the way everlasting."

Here, David, the author of this psalm, is asking God not only to search for roots of bitterness that might be planted in his heart but also to reveal the seeds of bitter thoughts floating down through the mind. We must remember that all roots begin with seeds. For us, these are anxious and provoking thoughts that have found their way down into the rich soil of our hearts. Once these anxious thoughts are firmly planted, bitter roots grow.

Not only do these bitter roots grow into weeds, they also produce more and more seeds that are cast into the winds of the mind and lead to yet more anxious thoughts. What a vicious cycle! David is asking God to stop the cycle and lead him in the way everlasting. How? David asks to be tested. "*Test me* and know my anxious thoughts. See if there is any offensive way in me."

Now, I wish I could tell you that each time God has tested me, I have passed with flying colors. However, more times than not, I've flat failed. When I was preparing to write this book, I prayed that God would reveal to me areas that I needed to work on. I gave a quick glance over the garden of my heart and things seemed well enough, so I proceeded. Now one thing I've failed to mention about weeds is that they can grow and hide in places you'd never think they could survive in—such as cracks in the sidewalks and the crevices of brick walls!

Feeling good about my heart's condition, I started clicking away at my computer's keyboard. Then came the fateful day of the mistaken drink. Now to give you a little background on the situation, when my husband and I first got married, bless his sweet-not-knowing-a-lot-about-women heart, he made some comments about my weight that resulted in bitter seeds, roots, and weeds galore.

(In his defense, I admit I provoked his comments with those questions all women feel compelled to ask: "This outfit makes my backside look big, doesn't it?" "This dress makes me look fat, doesn't it?")

Anyhow, some bitter roots dug in deep, and though I thought I'd pulled them all up, I guess a few still remained. I was busy writing away when my husband decided to bestow a great act of kindness upon me and bring me lunch. He called and asked what I wanted, and I gave him my precise order: a chicken sandwich with honey-mustard sauce and a Coke.

When he brought me my food, I noticed that the plastic lid of the drink had the little diet button pushed in, indicating it was Diet Coke, not the regular Coke I'd ordered. My throat tightened, my pulse ran wild, and instead of saying, "Thank you," I accused him of being insensitive and mean! I took the Diet Coke as a message that I should be drinking a diet drink because I was fat. But to him, it was a simple mistake with no hidden meaning at all.

Because of the early experiences in our marriage, I had allowed bitterness to take root in my heart, and when tested, all the weeds that came from that root reared their ugly heads. Now, if anyone else were to hand me a diet drink, I'd see it as a simple mistake. But because that bitter root was there against my husband, let's just say I failed my pop quiz and showed no gentleness that day.

What if God were to search you and test you? Would He find bitter thoughts forming seeds that blow through the winds of your mind? What would the garden of your heart look like? Do you have some weeding to do? Are there still others that are less obvious but no less destructive? Instead of pulling out the Weedwacker and hacking away at the flowers and stems, why not get right down to the root of the problem?

✍ *Spend some time recording in your journal the answers to these questions and any other thoughts you have about bitterness.*

Ask God to Teach You and Give You an Undivided Heart

Christ was the gentlest giant ever to walk the dusty roads of this earth. Though He had more reason than anyone to seek revenge and become bitter against those who mocked Him and wronged Him, He chose to show us how to respond with gentleness.

Jesus was fully God, with all power and authority over the earth. Jesus was also fully man, with feelings both emotional and physical. At times he showed His power and authority, as in the cleansing of the temple. But He also modeled an undivided, gentle heart when He walked the painful journey to the Cross. Put yourself in His shoes and feel the emotional and physical pain He must have felt.

Matthew 27:28–31 says,

> *They stripped him and put a scarlet robe on him, and then twisted together a crown of thorns and set it on his head. They put a staff in his right hand and knelt in front of him and mocked him. "Hail, king of the Jews!" they said. They spit on him, and took the staff and struck him on the head again and again. After they had mocked him, they took off the robe and put his own clothes on him. Then they led him away to crucify him.*

Verse 34 goes on to say, "There they offered Jesus wine to drink, mixed with gall; but after tasting it, he refused to drink it." Wine mixed with gall was a narcotic used to help deaden pain. Jesus knew this, and when He realized that the wine had the pain-killing and mind-numbing agent mixed in it, He refused it. Even extreme physical pain would not cause Jesus to abandon His cause. He had to be fully alert and aware so that gentleness could give his reply loud and clear.

And gentleness did just that. As Jesus died, He looked down

at those who mocked Him, the disciples who abandoned Him, and every one of us whose sin He bore in His body, and said, "Father, forgive them for they do not know what they are doing" (Luke 23:34). His one request to the Father while all this merciless abuse was taking place was that no bitter root be allowed to spoil the day. Gentleness blew bitterness and all his seeds, roots, and weeds from the scene with one breath of forgiveness.

Incidentally, Luke 23:34 concludes by saying, "And they divided up his clothes by casting lots." This verse was put here to make sure we know that prophecy was fulfilled, because it had been foretold that His garments would be divided and lots cast for them (Psalm 22:18). I can't help but wonder if Christ was thinking, *You can divide My clothes, but never will you divide My heart. I was sent here to bring the gentle answer to Satan's bitter revenge. I choose forgiveness; now what about you? My sweet child, what do you choose?*

May our answer be like Psalm 86:11–13:

Teach me your way, O Lord,
    and I will walk in your truth;
give me an undivided heart,
    that I may fear your name.
I will praise you, O Lord my God, with all my heart;
    I will glorify your name forever.
For great is your love toward me;
    you have delivered me from the depths of the grave.

✏ *Record in your journal your thoughts concerning Jesus' painful journey to the Cross. When we remember all that Christ has done for us—all He's delivered us from—how could we ever let any of the petty wrongdoings of others divide our hearts? Write from your heart your answer to this question. You may even wish to write a letter to the Lord asking Him to help you have an undivided heart.*

Choose the Gentle Response

We may be tempted to say, "It was easy for Jesus to choose the gentle response. After all, He's God!" But let's look at the story of Stephen—just an ordinary man, but a man filled with God's power. Acts 6:8–10 says,

> *Now Stephen, a man full of God's grace and power, did great wonders and miraculous signs among the people. Opposition arose, however, from members of the Synagogue of the Freedmen. . . . These men began to argue with Stephen, but they could not stand up against his wisdom or the Spirit by whom he spoke.*

The Scriptures tell of a conspiracy to get rid of Stephen. The synagogue leaders knew that Stephen was different. They saw God's power working in and through him. They heard the truth pour from his lips. They even saw something amazing about his face. Verse 15 says, "All who were sitting in the Sanhedrin looked intently at Stephen, and they saw that his face was like the face of an angel."

He, like Jesus, was being mocked, accused, questioned, and threatened. All these actions could provoke bitter revenge, yet through God's power Stephen had the gentle look of an angel!

The story continues as Stephen gives the religious leaders the message God had for them, which we read in Acts 7:51: "You stiff-necked people, with uncircumcised hearts and ears! You are just like your fathers: You always resist the Holy Spirit!" This rebuke by Stephen infuriated the Sanhedrin. Verses 54–55 tell us, "When they heard this, they were furious and gnashed their teeth at him. But Stephen, full of the Holy Spirit, looked up to heaven and saw the glory of God, and Jesus standing at the right hand of God."

The crowd dragged Stephen outside the city and began stoning him. In the midst of being stoned by the angry, bitter crowd,

Stephen cried out, "Lord, do not hold this sin against them" (v. 60). Then Stephen died.

Stephen was an ordinary man empowered by an extraordinary God. This same power given to Stephen is available to us through the Holy Spirit. Although we probably will never face the extreme situation Stephen did, we too will be asked to make a choice the next time we are wronged by another. Stephen chose the gentle response. Which will you choose?

Proverbs 15:1 says, "A gentle answer turns away wrath, but a harsh word stirs up anger." Since we know we can't control how other people act and react, we have to turn this verse inward. If we give a gentle answer, wrath will be turned away as soon as he knocks at our heart's door. But a harsh response from us stirs up anger and blows the doors of our hearts wide open—open to bitterness taking root and thriving.

The next time a friend hurts your feelings, your husband speaks harshly, your boss doesn't notice all that you have done but rather all that you haven't, your children turn up their noses at dinner, or one of the hundreds of other situations that may make you feel slighted . . . which will you choose? Will it be Satan's bitter revenge or God's gentle response?

I can't tell which response you might choose, but I can tell you what Jesus will do if you choose gentleness. Did you catch what Jesus did for Stephen in Acts 7:55–56? He stood at the right hand of the Father. Jesus normally sits at the right hand of the Father, but when Stephen chose gentleness even to the point of death, *Jesus gave him a standing ovation!*

✏ *Take time to really ponder Stephen's story and record your thoughts in your journal. What answer will you give the next time you feel wronged by another?*

*Choose the Ultimate Weed Killer (Forgiveness)
and the Ultimate Fertilizer (Faith)*

Once we have rid ourselves of these ugly weeds and have dug deep and pulled up the roots of bitterness, the job is not yet done. Ephesians 4:30–32 (italics added) tells us what must be done next. "Do not grieve the Holy Spirit of God, with whom you were sealed for the day of redemption. Get rid of all bitterness, rage and anger, brawling and slander, along with every form of malice. *Be kind and compassionate to one another, forgiving each other, just as in Christ God forgave you.*"

You see, once a weed has been pulled up by its root, the ground from which it came is broken apart and softened, ready for a new planting. Ephesians instructs us to plant kindness and compassion in the place of our bitter roots. Then beautiful blooms of gentleness can grow and spread and redefine your heart's garden. But forgiveness plays a big part in this verse as well. That is where the real secret to having a weed-free garden lies.

After a few years of struggling to kill the weeds in our yard and keep the grass alive, my husband and I discovered a wonderful product called "Weed 'n' Feed." Now, instead of laboriously pulling up weeds and replanting grass seed all the time, we simply fertilize the yard with this marvelous product. It serves as a weed killer and weed preventer, and it even fertilizes our grass.

Could there be such a similar spiritual remedy? There is. Forgiveness is the ultimate killer of bitter seeds, roots, and weeds. If we develop an attitude of forgiveness, bitterness will never even have a chance to take root in our hearts. Forgiveness turns bitterness into joy as we have the opportunity to give to others as Christ has given to us. Remember, as Matthew 6:15 instructs, if we do not forgive others, our Father will not forgive us!

As forgiveness keeps your heart's garden free of weeds, faith is the best fertilizer for beautiful things to grow and flourish. Faith feeds the flowers of love, joy, peace, patience, kindness, goodness, gentleness, and self-control. The stronger your faith, the more flowers that can be produced. Now if you've spent any time at all in a garden, you know that a fruit-producing branch always announces the arrival of fruit with beautiful flowers first. As faith fertilizes, flowers grow and then the fruit of the spirit bursts forth.

A HEART RENEWED

Days after their daughter was shot to death, Beth Nimmo and Darrell Scott laid Rachel to rest in a white coffin signed by her family and friends. It would have been completely understandable for these parents to harbor fury in their hearts. They could have been bitter and angry, seeking revenge on the person who sold guns to the minors who used them to shoot their child, on the parents of the killers, or most understandably, on the killers themselves, Eric Harris and Dylan Klebold. Yet in the dedication to their book about Rachel, after writing small memorials for those who lost their lives at Columbine, they wrote these words, "The two perpetrators of these horrible killings took their own lives that tragic day. We ask that you pray for the Klebold and Harris families, who have been subjected to their own unimaginable grief."[2]

If anyone had reason to be bitter, Beth Nimmo and Darrell Scott certainly did. I'm sure there have been times since Rachel's death when it must have seemed like the only sensible reaction. Yet, they have chosen to focus their energies on letting God bring good out of their loss. Filling themselves with hatred and rage would have done nothing but stoke their torment. After all, it was the wild, festering bitterness that filled the killers that sent Rachel to the grave. Feeding this type of hatred would not bring their daughter back; it would only tarnish the precious legacy she left behind.

In the closing words of their book, Beth and Darrell shared

their thoughts on forgiveness and how they have each made their way to gentle choices.

Beth: "In the year since Rachel's death, I have found it difficult to follow Christ's command to forgive the killers. Forgiveness has been a daily battle for me. Sometimes it has even been a moment-by-moment struggle. From the beginning I have asked the Lord to give me real forgiveness for Eric and Dylan, but that desire is repeatedly tested. . . . One year after Rachel's death, forgiveness is not a one-time act of my will, but it's a choice I make on an on-going basis. I choose constantly to lay down my pain because I trust God to do something incredibly beautiful through all this."[3]

Darrell: "I turned to the end of her last diary and could not believe what was staring up at me from that final page! A drawing of a rose with a stream of tears that were watering a rose. Later someone pointed out to me that there were thirteen clear tears falling from her eyes before they touched the rose and turned into what looked like blood drops. There were of course thirteen victims of the two murderers."[4]

Several weeks after seeing Rachel's drawing for the first time, Darrell told the story of the rose at a speaking engagement. Afterward, a girl handed him her Bible, opened to Jeremiah 31:15–17 (NASB):

Thus says the Lord,
"A voice is heard in Ramah,
Lamentation and bitter weeping.
Rachel is weeping for her children;
She refuses to be comforted for her children,
Because they are no more."
Thus says the Lord,

"Restrain your voice from weeping,
And your eyes from tears;
For your work shall be rewarded," declares the Lord,
"And they will return from the land of the enemy.
There is hope for your future," declares the Lord,
"And your children shall return to their own territory."

Darrell says,

When I read these words, the door of closure slammed shut in my spirit. I knew from that moment that Rachel's death was not in vain. I knew this teacher and twelve students were going to have an eternal impact on the lives of many people. I knew the Columbine flower Rachel had drawn represented the tragedy out of which the youth of this generation (the rose) would emerge, anointed by the very tears of God that were pictured flowing from Rachel's eyes. This tragedy will be turned into triumph by the grace of God![5]

This is such an amazing story exemplifying how the ultimate weed killers, forgiveness and faith, work together to help people choose a gentle response instead of bitterness. Although many of us will never be asked to make the choice at the level Rachel's parents have had to, *we will still have to make the choice.* For in differing degrees we all have and will continue to experience deep hurts that come our way.

Remember: God never wastes a hurt if we give it to Him. He certainly hasn't in Rachel's case, and He won't in yours either.

DISCUSSION QUESTIONS

1. Hebrews 12:15 says, "See to it that no one misses the grace of God and that no bitter root grows up to cause trouble and defile many." What does it mean to say that a bitter root could "cause trouble and defile many"?

2. Why is it useless to ask the "If only" questions?

3. Why is it important to pray Psalm 139:23–24, "Search me, O God, and know my heart; test me and know my anxious thoughts. See if there is any offensive way in me, and lead me in the way everlasting?"

4. Discuss this statement: "Jesus was also fully man, with feelings both emotional and physical. At times He showed His power and authority, as in the cleansing of the temple. But He also modeled for us an undivided gentle heart when He walked the painful journey to the Cross. Put yourself in His shoes and consider the emotional and physical pain He must have felt."

5. What was it that gave Stephen the resolve and strength to choose the gentle response? Discuss Jesus' reaction to Stephen's actions. How does this affect you personally?

6. What was your favorite Scripture in this chapter, and how did it impact you?

7. How does forgiveness free us? Why is forgiveness so important? If anyone has a personal testimony to share relating to this chapter, please do so.

CHAPTER NINE

ADDICTION IS SATAN'S PLEASURE
SELF-CONTROL IS GOD'S REPLY

He reached down from on high and took hold of me;
he drew me out of deep waters.
He rescued me from my powerful enemy,
from my foes who were too strong for me.
They confronted me in the day of my disaster,
but the LORD was my support.
He brought me out into a spacious place;
he rescued me because he delighted in me.

❖

PSALM 18:16–19

The air was electric with excitement. Her white dress was stunning. The scent of fresh flowers lingered and mixed with heavenly music delighting the senses of the many guests. It was her day, a day she had dreamed about all her life. Finally, she'd met a wonderful man, and now they would forever be joined as husband and wife. Everyone she loved was there to share in this joyous occasion. Well, almost everyone.

All the beauty seemed to swirl around her as her mind raced to a simple tree atop Old Rags Mountain. This was a tree her father had planted in loving memory of his best friend, who'd committed suicide there. But it wasn't really the tree that kept drawing her heart's attention; it was her father's ashes scattered there. He'd ended his own life in the same place two years after his friend. That one bullet had not only ripped through the flesh of her father, but in a way it had destroyed Sheila as well. Now, four years later, there would be no last embrace as they headed down the aisle together . . . no father's shaky voice to say he gives this woman to be wed . . . and no dancing with her daddy.

Sheila had loved her father. Her life was always an adventure with him. Once, when Sheila was anxious about a history exam, he'd asked her what time she would be taking the test. She told him, and he promised to be thinking of her right at that moment. To her surprise, soon after she'd begun to take the test, her name was called over the school's intercom. When she got to the office, her father was on the telephone. He wanted her to know he was thinking of her . . . and to see if she needed help with some of the answers!

This and so many other memories now flooded this daddy's girl's heart.

Oh, how she missed him. What could she have done differently? Was there something she could have said? She knew her dad's happiness held a dark side of infidelities and alcoholism. Could she have somehow reached him? All of that was beyond her control now. He was gone.

As she recounted the story for me, she said, "My father shot himself on top of a mountain. Then I was left walking in the dark valley below with all the scars, the blaming, and the whys." Sheila's heart felt an emptiness that had to be filled. That's when Satan reared his ugly head and offered her his answer to control: his pleasure, addiction.

It did not take long for this small-framed girl to get down to eighty-five pounds. Sheila simply stopped eating, which gave her the sense of control she desperately longed for. When people became alarmed at her obvious drop in weight, anorexia's sister, bulimia, was the answer. Secrecy is a must for most addictions, and eating disorders are no different. Bulimia allowed her to eat in front of suspecting eyes and then purge her body in secret.

The bingeing and purging cycle that at first made her feel such a sense of control was now controlling her. She kept everyone at a safe distance. If friends or relatives threatened her secret by getting too close, she pushed them away. Deception was now her life. She became obsessed with the day-to-day control of her secret. Even when she met her husband-to-be, Steve, she kept this part of her life from him.

Now she was dancing to the sad tune of a painful secret at her wedding instead of the joyous songs everyone else heard. Oh, her feet seemed to keep perfect rhythm that night. Even her smiling face kept up the routine. But behind the mask and behind the walls, her heart was out of step with the joy she should have been feeling.

UNLOCKING ADDICTIONS

Of all the topics in this book, the subject of addiction was one I questioned addressing. Because she is a dear friend, I knew Sheila's story, yet I hadn't heard much about addictions from the women I teach at church or speak to at conferences. Well, God dispelled my reluctance with one piercing thought. I felt God say to my heart, "The reason you don't hear much about them is because they are held in secret. They are Satan's secret pleasure, Lysa."

And God did not just leave me to wonder about this thought. As He is so faithful to do, He confirmed what He was saying to me a few short weeks later at a speaking engagement. I was restless the night before I was to speak, because I felt God was telling me to take nothing to the podium but my Bible. The thought persisted throughout the night and all the next day. Finally, I found myself sitting in the church waiting to walk to the front.

I couldn't believe God was asking me to leave my notes on the pew. I knew it was God speaking to me, but I wrestled with what He was asking of me. Finally, as the woman up front introduced me, I told God that He had won, and I left my notes behind. Carrying only my Bible—and butterflies in my heart and stomach—I walked forward.

I asked my listeners to turn over the outlines they held, because God wanted me to speak on something different. Then for the next two hours God poured His comfort through me and touched souls like I'd never seen before. The heart of the message that day was this: Though we all fail Jesus at times, that doesn't make us failures. God's grace is big enough to cover any sin. At the end of our time together, four women accepted Christ as Lord and Savior and many others recommitted their hearts to Him.

After the conference ended, I understood why God had a special message for these special women. Almost every woman in the audience was an addict of one kind or another, living in a group home. Seeing their faces during the conference, I could tell life had been hard on some, but their painful circumstances were not obvious from their appearances.

Afterward, when I toured the group home where many of them lived, I started to understand who God was reaching out to that day. Some women had been addicted to drugs and sold their bodies for just one more high. Others had gotten lost in a daze of alcohol, so everything had been taken from them, including their children. Each story's circumstances varied, but a common thread tied them all together.

They were hurting. Satan had enticed them to buy into his pleasures to fill the longings of their hearts, and as a result, their lives were torn to shreds. The fruit of self-control that comes with having God's Spirit in you was what they needed. They had all tried to beat their addictions on their own, but moments of weakness and rationalization drew them back. With each step backward, hope of escape became more distant. Some did not even believe hope still existed.

✎ *Have you ever been in a similar place? Write about it in your journal.*

As they learned more about Jesus and how to have a growing relationship with Him, these women grasped new hope. It was truly miraculous. It was like seeing God's light engulf Satan's darkness, as one by one their eyes brightened, their spirits lifted, and heaven reclaimed some of its own. I realized that day that it was only by the grace of God that I was the speaker and not sitting in the audience myself.

Not one of us has escaped Satan's enticements. Not one of us is incapable of being deceived. Only when we are constantly aware of the control that is ours because the Holy Spirit resides in us can we walk past temptation's offerings and look the other way.

Addictions are powerful, my friend. They grab their victims in such subtle ways that you hardly know you're snagged until it is too late. Dr. Alan Leshner, director of the National Institute on Drug Abuse (NIDA), in an article published by *Newsweek,* said, "Addiction affects every aspect of an individual's interaction with the world."[1]

We've all heard the tragic stories. A teen tries a drug just one time to be cool in front of his friends, and five months later he's a full-blown addict. His whole life revolves around his body's cravings for more and more of the drug. He lies and steals from his parents and disregards the future that once looked so bright.

A man in his late forties befriends a woman at work. She is attractive and soothes the ache he sometimes feels when he thinks about not being so young anymore. Before long he's addicted to the feeling he has when he's with her. It consumes his thought life and, before long, leads to an affair. His wife and family, once so precious to him, are left in the wake of his destructive pursuit.

A woman who finds herself overwhelmed with the demands of being a wife and a mother decides to take the edge off her nerves and have a drink. Soon one drink becomes two, and then three, and then more than she can keep track of. She is lost in a haze of drunkenness and denial that prevents her from caring for herself—much less her child. Then, during a moment of soberness, she finds a terrible bruise on her little one. She is horrified to realize the black-and-blue handprint is her very own.

Addictions can be as full-blown as those cases or subtler and less severe. They can grip anyone. But we still must call sin *sin* and expose it for what it is. Anything that misses the mark of God's best for us is sin. Anything that lures us away from the Holy Spirit's control in our lives is a type of addiction.

In an interview, Joann Condie, a Licensed Professional Counselor with Focus on the Family, revealed a startling truth about Christians locked in addictions when she said, "Christians who are addicts are some of the most hurting people with the biggest smiles hiding their pain."[2] Have you ever been one of these "smiling" people?

✎ *If you are in this place right now, write the name of one person in whom you could confide. If you are not in this place now, journal ways to reach out to those who may be hurting.*

Webster's New World Dictionary defines an addict as "one who gives himself up to a strong habit." Please notice the word *strong* there. Remember, Satan is crafty and cunning and the master of strongholds. Any habit that holds your attention more than God does is an addiction and must be dealt with.

So here we stand with our strong habit in our arms. One part of us longs to toss it away and let its sting be gone forever, but another part wants to hold on to its familiar comforts. The teen wonders what his body will do without the drug's high. The man wonders if his arms could ever be filled with as much satisfaction as that woman seems to give him. And the young mother wonders how she'll calm her edgy nerves without the liquor. They desperately wonder, *What will Jesus do with this addiction? Can He really fill my emptiness?*

Satan is scrambling to keep his victim locked in this stronghold. He pulls out all the stops as he feeds lies into his victims' minds, lies specifically designed for each one's insecurities and hurts. Quickly, he slithers ever so close and says, "Don't listen to Jesus. Only I can satisfy you with my pleasuresssssss. He won't heal you. You're too far into this thing. You're an addict, remember, *an addict.* God is so busy attending to all the good people of this world—do you really think He has time for little ol' you? Hisssss, Hissss."

SELF-CONTROL IS GOD'S REPLY

Suddenly, Jesus steps right out of Mark 8:33 and says, "Get behind me, Satan! . . . You do not have in mind the things of God, but the things of men." Then He calls out to you, "If anyone would come after me, he must deny himself and take up his cross and follow me" (v. 34).

Now, before you decide which path you will choose, I must draw your attention to two fundamental truths here. Remember, it is the truth that will set you free, so we must explore truth to its fullest. To get to the full truth, we must ask why Jesus would command Satan to get behind Him. Inside the answer to this question we will find our two fundamental points.

First, Jesus told Satan to get behind Him because it is Satan's sin that separates you and Jesus. Satan's very name, in the original

Greek, means "one who casts either himself or something between two in order to separate them." Jesus is longing to reach out and grab hold of you. He's longing to touch your wounds with His healing hands and whisper truths of love and acceptance into your soul. But something has been cast between you for the sole purpose of separating you from your Redeemer. So, Jesus commands the *separation* away by commanding the *separator* away.

The second fundamental we must look at is this: Jesus commands Satan *because He can*. Satan trembles when God speaks. Satan not only trembles, but he leaves when Jesus commands him to leave. You see, Satan is a defeated foe. He has no power when God commands. God is in control.

What does this mean for you and me? It means that if you have accepted Jesus as Lord of your life, and if it is He who reigns supreme in your heart, then you have His power and control in you. That's self-control's reply. We have been given the Holy Spirit to indwell us, and self-control is one of the fruits that testify to the Spirit's presence. We too can look Satan's addictions and sinful pleasures squarely in the eyes and say, "Get behind me!"

Now rest assured that self-control's reply does not just leave us there, hoping it works. No, Jesus goes on in verse 34 to instruct us what to do after we command evil away.

Notice that at the beginning of this verse Jesus calls the crowd and His disciples to hear what He is about to say. Because of His many miracles, some performed that very day (the feeding of the four thousand and the healing of the blind man), Jesus has established Himself as the Great Provider and the Great Physician. But He is more than a provider of food to ease our physical hunger and a healer of broken bodies. His ultimate mission is to fill us with Himself so that our spiritual hunger will be met and to touch our broken hearts so that our very souls can be healed.

✐ *Journal your thoughts about Jesus as your healer.*

I can just hear His heart pleading for the people to listen to what He is about to say. They had seen Him work miracles in the physical realm; now it was time to go to the next level and touch on eternity. Jesus told them—and tells us—that if anyone wants to come after Him, he or she must do three things.

First, we are to deny ourselves. We must deny that we have any ability on our own to fill the hunger in our souls and mend our broken hearts. Only Jesus, who calls Himself the Bread of Life and the Living Water, can pour Himself into our souls and fill up our every empty nook and cranny. Only His touch can heal us. Everything we try to fill ourselves up with will fall short.

We must also deny ourselves the temporary pleasure of trying to fill ourselves. Don't rush over that last sentence. Read it again: *We must also deny ourselves the temporary pleasure of trying.* Filling our bodies with immoral sexual encounters, drugs, alcohol, food, perfectionism, or any one of many addictions, may bring us moments of temporary pleasure. But I can guarantee, because I've been there, that this type of pleasure is fleeting and followed by a tremendous amount of pain. To follow after Christ means to give Him supreme authority over our hearts and leave the filling and the healing up to Him.

✑ *Journal some practical ways you can do this in your life.*

Second, we must take up our cross. This same story told in the ninth chapter of Luke says, "If anyone would come after me, he must deny himself and take up his cross daily" (v. 23). To understand this, we must understand what Jesus did when He took up His cross. He died. But then He rose again, as a new being. This is where we must turn to 2 Corinthians 5:17, which says, "Therefore, if anyone is in Christ, he is a new creation; the old has gone, the new has come!" To take up your cross means to crucify your old self with its habits, thought patterns, and addictions.

For many of us that will be a daily process as the old self tries to rear its ugly head. We are new creations of our Living Savior, and we must claim our new identities daily. To do this we must form new habits and thought patterns to replace the old.

Romans 12:1–2 sums it up well: "Therefore, I urge you, brothers, in view of God's mercy, to offer your bodies as living sacrifices, holy and pleasing to God—this is your spiritual act of worship. Do not conform any longer to the pattern of this world, but be transformed by the renewing of your mind." We must stop here because the rest of this verse carries us into the third instruction of Christ.

✐ *Now, write in your journal how you can take up your cross daily.*

The third thing Christ instructs us to do is to follow Him. So, to continue with the last part of Romans 12:2, "Then you will be able to test and approve what God's will is—his good, pleasing and perfect will." You see, to follow Christ, really follow Him, you must not only know the Father's will, but you must also *follow* it.

That is when you will notice that you are right in step with His Son. That is when you will know you are dancing to the same tune. That is when the Holy Spirit's fruit of self-control whispers in your ear this sweet reply: "Here I am, I have come—it is written about me in the scroll." And you look at the face of your eternal Beloved and say, "I desire to do your will, O my God; your law is within my heart" (Psalm 40:7–8).

✐ *Record Psalm 40:7–8 in your journal.*

Hold on to the promise, "Being confident of this, that he who began a good work *in* you will carry it on to completion until the day of Christ Jesus" (Philippians 1:6). God began His good work *for* you when Jesus died on the cross, allowing forgiveness for all sin—past, present, and future. His work began in you the day you accepted Jesus as your personal Lord and Savior. This good work never stops and will be complete *only* when we meet Jesus face-to-face.

Rest assured that when God starts His work in your life, He *will* complete it! "When you are discouraged, remember that God won't give up on you. . . . When you feel incomplete, unfinished, or distressed by your shortcomings, remember God's promise and provision. Don't let your present condition rob you of the joy of knowing Christ or keep you from growing closer to him."[3]

➱ *Journal the wonderful hope this gives you.*

Overcoming an addiction is not something you can do in your own strength. Joann Condie says, "What feeds the addiction cycle more than anything is isolation. It's the divide and conquer theory. If Satan can convince you that you're a second-class Christian and there's no safe person to confide in, then hopelessness sets in."[4] People make the mistake of thinking, *If only I were more disciplined, or had a stronger will, then I could knock this thing.* Don't let yourself fall into the trap of putting this kind of pressure on yourself. It is only through God's strength that anyone can overcome an addiction. So what is your responsibility in all of this? Determine to fill yourself with more and more of God and seek the necessary Christian professional help you need.

This point became evident to me one day while I stood washing dishes in the kitchen sink. I started by turning the water on and spraying it over the dirty plates, utensils, and cups. One cup that was filled with red juice caught my eye. As I poured more and more water into it, slowly but surely the red juice dissipated and finally was gone altogether. Sometimes this is how our addiction will be cured by Jesus. The more His Living Water pours into us, the less room there will be for the junk of this world. It's an exchange. Instead of the food, alcohol, or drugs, Jesus becomes our fulfillment. We'll crave His touch. We'll crave His words. We'll crave to be filled with Him alone.

In some cases, God's perfect plan for a person is an instant miraculous healing, as you will see in the conclusion of Sheila's story. Other times God's perfect plan is to take a person on a journey of healing with a godly professional counselor to whom God has given an extra measure of wisdom and insight. This journey to healing is often the best process for people with deep wounds stemming from a past hurtful relationship. A safe relationship with a Christian counselor can be incredibly beneficial.

Why Christian counseling? Because a person must find healing for body, mind, spirit, and soul. Only a Christian counselor can touch on all these areas. The *Newsweek* article on addictions mentioned earlier reported on cures for addictions solely in the physical realm.

> Overcoming addiction is never simple. The risk of relapse is so high—roughly half of all patients fall off the wagon within a year of detoxification—that many health professionals consider treatment a waste of time. When researchers at California's Kaiser Permanente health plan surveyed doctors and nurses a few years ago, most viewed medical intervention as "ineffective" and "inappropriate."[5]

This is why it is so important to seek a counselor that can address healing at every level, especially the soul. Also, please don't ever feel that if your healing isn't instant, then you're less of a Christian or have fewer chances for complete healing. Your healing will be a miraculous work of God no matter which path you may have to travel. Rest assured, the place you are in now is not where you will be forever unless you choose not to allow God to carry you to His place of healing.

For more information on Christian counseling, call Focus on the Family at: 1–800–A–FAMILY and ask for the counseling department. They offer a wealth of information, hope, and healing.

A HEART RENEWED

Sheila's struggle with anorexia and bulimia lasted three more long and painful years. During that time she kept looking for an escape and was forever manipulating and designing a cure for her addiction. Nothing she did helped.

Then Jesus mercifully revealed His healing power to her. He spoke personally to her heart and said, "I want you free." She had known Him as Savior but never as the Great Physician. She had been walking in and out of church for many years carrying the burden of her painful secret. That day she finally heard His call, trusted His tender touch, and accepted His loving pursuit of her. Sheila said,

I never knew Jesus could possibly love me that much. It was like Jesus stepped in front of Satan, picked me up, and brought me into His light. It was then that I saw myself in chains and bondage. I wanted out of those chains! I realized I had been deceived by Satan, and I knew in my heart that I desperately wanted to be released from him. Though I was saved and walking with Jesus, I had been deceived. Now the light of truth was drawing me and I wanted His love and healing power as I had never wanted anything else in my life.

I realized not only that I had been hurting myself, I had been sinning against God. I was serving another, obsessed with something, and abusing His temple. My husband and I had been trying for a long time to have a baby, and now I knew why I wasn't pregnant. I was killing myself.

When Sheila connected Jesus' truth to the longing within her, Satan's lies were exposed. She saw her addiction for what it really was—a way to keep her from the ultimate satisfaction of a passionate relationship with the Great Lover of her soul. She discovered the only way to fill her soul's emptiness was with the One who created her, formed her, and placed within her a longing for Him.

Finally, she realized nothing Satan had to offer could ever bring her true and lasting happiness. She surrendered her whole heart—even the secret places—to the Master Healer and began a new waltz with Jesus.

In the presence of His flawless love, the dry places of her heart were filled to overflowing. Her addiction was conquered and Sheila was set free. Now she looks forward to another kind of wedding where the Great Bridegroom will return to claim her as His bride.

Then she will have that wedding dance with her Heavenly Daddy, a dance she missed with her earthly daddy. As Sheila says, "I will take the hand that created me. I will hold the palm that has my name written on it. I will be in the arms I have run to many times. I will dance on the feet that have guided me to all truth. I will look into the eyes that have watched me every second of my life. I will touch the face of love and dance down streets of gold."

A NOTE FROM SHEILA'S HEART TO YOURS

My dear friend,

Satan lies to us about achieving happiness in life. Happiness from him is money, looks, cars, homes, clothes, religion, success, prestige, recognition, fame, people-pleasing, popularity, or addictions. I was enjoying that satisfaction at times only because I was deceived. Therefore, I was being kept from the ultimate satisfaction of knowing the fullness of my Savior's love.

Satan's goal is to keep you away from Jesus if you don't know Him, or to render you ineffective if you do know Him. You may be deceived with drugs, alcohol, sex, food, perfectionism, or any one of the hundreds of other addictions Satan offers. Whatever it might be, it's bondage, and you are being kept from the greatest satisfaction of all: knowing Jesus intimately. You cannot live a full life without allowing Jesus Christ to be your everything. Worldly things will not make you happy. There is an emptiness in your soul that only God can fill.

You can try to fit other things in there, but they simply won't fill you. That piece of the puzzle to your heart is God's and His alone. He has the exclusive rights to it. He holds the patent because He made you. "Is he not your Father, your Creator, who made you and formed you?" (Deuteronomy 32:6). He chose you to be His. "Yet to all who received him, to those who believed in his name, he gave the right to become children of God—children born not of natural descent, nor of human decision or a husband's will, but born of God" (John 1:12–13). He is drawing you to Him. "No one can come to me unless the Father who sent me draws him, and I will raise him up at the last day "(John 6:44). The ultimate decision is yours. "Submit yourselves, then, to God. Resist the devil, and he will flee from you. Come near to God and he will come near to you" (James 4:7–8).

I pray these Scriptures that are so dear to me will touch your soul and draw you out of whatever darkness you are in. His light is wonderful. I feel like a ballerina I once heard about who was part of the New York City Ballet. She was described by some critics as easily distracted by a lack of confidence. Then Mikhail Baryshnikov chose her as his partner, and her reviews changed to "exhilarating," "sensational," and even "breathtaking!" We have been chosen by the Master to be His partner. Let's follow His lead, mimic His steps, take His control for our very own, and dance, yes dance in His light!

In His love,
Sheila Mangum

DISCUSSION QUESTIONS

1. Do you think we all struggle with addictions to varying degrees?

2. Why are addictions "Satan's pleasure"?

3. Why is keeping addictions secret so very dangerous? Why is it so important to not be isolated?

4. Discuss Joann Condie's comment, "Christians who are addicts are some of the most hurting people with the biggest smiles hiding their pain."

5. What are some practical ways you can take up your cross daily? How could this help bad habits—or addictions?

6. What was your favorite passage of Scripture in this section? How did God speak to your heart through this verse?

CONCLUSION

I wrote this conclusion in my hometown, a most appropriate place to compose these final words. You see, so much of what happened to me early in life, events that helped shape the person I've become, happened in this place. My quest for freedom started when I was a young girl. I desperately wanted to be free of the pain in my heart, but I didn't know how. I captured those young, hurting feelings in poems I wrote. As I read some of them again, I was struck by the fact that I knew there was a key that could unlock my pain, but I didn't know where to find it. I talked about this key in several of those early writings. One poem I wrote when I was thirteen is titled "Dreams."

As the tides roll in and shells scamper about,
children run around trying to rescue them before they once again roll out.
That's how dreams are, and the ones you want to keep
seem to just roll away locked into the ocean deep.
Though there's always a chance you'll find the key,
you run along the shore watching more and more dreams
being carried out to sea.

Besides reading some of my old poetry, I also took a walk with my mom in the neighborhood where I spent many of my young years. As we ventured past the house that was once our home, we reminisced about old times and past neighbors. But we didn't talk about all the hurt that once filled the walls of that old blue house. We didn't have to because the hurts have changed. Once those wounds were raw and deep, but now, miraculously, they have changed from ugly scars into beautiful markings. These marks on my soul are precious to me, because they allow me to trace the touch of the Master's hand upon my life.

I can honestly say that I would not have it any other way. I would not wish away a single tear I've shed, for I know what it feels like to have Jesus wipe my face. I would not wish away any of the heartbreak, for I know what it is like for God to put the pieces back together and create in me a stronger heart. I would not wish away all the times I felt unloved by others, for they have drawn me closer to the Great Lover of my soul. I would not wish away a single moment of the valleys I've traveled in, for it is in those low places that my soul found God's strength to climb to the high places.

Habakkuk 3:19 says, "The Lord God is my strength, and He has made my feet like hinds' feet, and makes me walk on my high places" (NASB). In the book named for this verse, *Hinds' Feet on High Places,* author Hannah Hurnard recounts a story about a character named Much-Afraid and her journey to the High Places. In one particularly moving scene, Much-Afraid and the loving Shepherd are talking about her journey:

> Poor Much-Afraid, who knew she had been slipping and stumbling in the most dreadful way, indeed worse than at any other time, flushed painfully all over her face. She said nothing, only looked at him almost reproachfully. "Much-Afraid," said he very gently in answer to that look, "don't you know by now that I never think of you as you are now but as you will be when I have

brought you to the Kingdom of Love and washed you from all the stains and defilements of the journey? If I come along behind you and notice that you are finding the way especially difficult, and are suffering from slips and falls, it only makes me think of what you will be like when you are with me, leaping and skipping on the High Places."[1]

In one of the final chapters, Much-Afraid finally reaches the first slopes of the Kingdom of Love.

She never tired of looking from the glorious new viewpoint on the first slopes of the Kingdom of Love and seeing it all from a new perspective. What she could see and could take in almost intoxicated her with joy and thanksgiving, and sometimes even with inexpressible relief. Things which she had thought dark and terrible and which had made her tremble as she looked up from the Valley because they had seemed so alien to any part of the Realm of Love were now seen to be parts of a great and wonderful whole.[2]

The purpose of this book is not at all to point out places where your slips and falls have occurred, but rather to draw your heart to a place of wonderful healing. For I know that when we pursue healing, we gain new perspective. I hope that as you have worked your way through these pages, your heart has learned to be brave enough and your mind open enough to truly experience God as never before. I pray that your journey from here is wild and wonderful and that you never forget that you are whole and holy by His love. As Ephesians 1:4–6 tells us, "He chose us in him before the creation of the world to be holy and blameless in his sight. In love he predestined us to be adopted as his sons through Jesus Christ, in accordance with his pleasure and will—to the praise of his glorious grace, which he has freely given us in the One he loves."

I also hope that you've gained a deeper desire to seek God with all your heart. In Jeremiah 29:13–14 we read, "'You will seek me and find me when you seek me with all your heart. I will be found by you,' declares the LORD, 'and will bring you back from captivity.'" I pray that there are no more secret places you are hiding from Him and no more dark places of pain you withhold from the Master's touch. When we expose those hidden places to Him, He will reveal the way out of captivity. Whether it is through His instantaneous healing or through a godly counselor He brings your way, you can find freedom. Also, it is only through seeking God with your whole heart that you can most purely exemplify to others His love, joy, peace, patience, kindness, goodness, faithfulness, gentleness, and self-control.

You probably noticed that as we worked through God's responses in each of the chapters, they followed the pattern of the fruit of the Spirit as found in Galatians 5:22. This was not by chance. For to discover the glorious living (as mentioned in the verses from Ephesians above) we must seek to become living proof that Christ lives and resides in us and works through us.

We must let God unlock Satan's vices of shame, despair, fear, discontentment, loneliness, insecurity, doubt, bitterness, and addictions because it is completely beyond human understanding how one can be truly set free. Our lives will be a living testimony to others of God's power. Others will want to know how to join us on our journey to the high places. What joy there is in sharing the journey with others! By exemplifying love, joy, peace, patience, kindness, faithfulness, gentleness, and self-control we can show, not just tell, the world about the One who gives us the strength to climb and the glory to be found at the journey's end.

Thank you for joining me on this adventure. I could say that this is now where our journey ends, but because Jesus holds the key to your heart, this is actually where the journey truly begins.

✐ *Pull out your journal one last time and record what God has done in your heart through this study. You may want to have one last group discussion in which you share your testimonies.*

THE KEY

There once was a little princess who lived in a small cottage in the mountain forest. Her cozy home was nestled between meadows of colorful wildflowers and tall trees. Though beautiful, it was hardly a typical castle for a princess.

You see, this princess did not know she was of royal descent. When she looked at her reflection in the mountain streams and valley rain puddles, she saw a simple little girl. Yet, she did own one thing that made her different. Under her bed in a simple gold box, she had letters, amazing letters. The little princess loved pulling her box out and spreading the letters all over the floor. Though she barely understood the words they contained, they brought her a wonderful sense of love and comfort. Sometimes her mother would pull out the letters that told stories, and the two of them would cuddle up and let their minds imagine how the characters might have looked and what life lessons their stories taught.

One day the little princess was playing down by the stream when suddenly a strange snake slithered near her. The girl was not frightened by the creature, but rather intrigued, so she stepped toward it to get a better look.

Much to her surprise, the snake spoke. "Have you ever visited the caverns on the other side of the meadow down in the deep valley?"

"No. Mother warned me that it is not safe for little girls to wander that far from home alone," she replied.

"Well, you wouldn't be alone if I went with you. It sure is fun," the snake said with a sly smile and a slight hiss.

"I don't know if my mother would like that. I probably should ask her first," the little princess said with a bit of hesitation in her voice.

"Oh, but if you ask her first, you'll ruin the surprise. You see, there are beautiful flowers that grow in the deep valley and amazing jewels in the caverns. Wouldn't you like to make your mother happy and find some of these special gifts for her?"

"Oh," sighed the little princess. "My mother is so sweet, and I'd love to find her something special. I guess it would be fine just this once."

The snake slithered even closer to the little princess. "Good, good, you will be so glad. There is beauty in those caverns that you've never seen before." The little girl followed the snake off across the meadow and down into the deep valley.

The deep valley and its dark caverns held none of the beauty and wonder the snake promised. The thrill of adventure was quickly replaced by the sting of deception. The little princess ran home but decided not to tell her mom about the events of her day. Instead, she opened a little closet in her heart and stuffed the hurt inside. She locked shame's door and hid the key in her pocket.

That night when her mother came to tuck her into bed, the little princess did not want to read the letters. After her mother kissed her goodnight and left the room, a tear trickled down her small, tender cheek.

Over the years the snake's unexpected visits became more and more frequent. His adventures promised wonderful fun but always ended the same way. More closets were opened in the little princess' heart. More hurtful experiences were locked away. More and more tears stained her pillow. She desired to read her letters less and less, until one day she forgot about them altogether. The once carefree and happy little girl who ran through the meadows, climbed the trees, and gazed up at the stars dreaming beautiful dreams was lost.

Just as time always does, it marched on and on. The little feet that once gaily skipped through the small country cottage were replaced by the tired step of a heavyhearted lady. Routine became her friend; busyness, her companion. The constant distraction of things to do helped numb the troubles in her heart.

Over the years it became easier and easier to hide behind a mask of pleasantries and surface exchanges whenever she dealt with people. She preferred to keep her distance from them, but her busyness demanded interaction. Oh, how she feared someone might somehow catch a glimpse of her imperfections. She was sure none of them had ever been visited by the snake. Or if they had, surely they hadn't made the same mistakes she had. Most of the time she kept up her charade and smiled and laughed and pretended everything was just fine.

It was when she climbed into bed at night, when routine and busyness left her, that she heard the familiar cry. It wasn't a painful cry or even a particularly urgent one, but it was a still, small voice that patiently called her name. Where did it come from? She knew it was a voice she had heard as a child, but she couldn't remember how to answer it. Sobs that made her chest rise and fall in quick, deep shudders soon drowned out the voice and eventually sleep would overtake her.

One night, after her pillow had been saturated with her tears and sleep comforted her once more, she dreamed of being in a room with a huge pot of melted gold. A man stood over the pot, stirring and stirring. The fire beneath the pot was intense enough to melt the gold and cause something inside the gold to rise to the surface. Then the man would scrape the sludgelike substance off, cast it aside, and stare down into the pot. After gazing intently for a little while, he began stirring again and the whole process started over.

Intrigued by what she saw, she stepped a little closer. Suddenly, something familiar caught her eye. On a stool beside the man was a simple gold box filled with letters. Every now and then, he would stop stirring and read a letter out loud over the pot. The box was familiar, but when she heard the words contained in the letters, she remembered the wisdom, comfort, and amazing stories and realized they were her letters. She ran over to the man and asked him where he'd found them. He smiled gently and said, "My dear, your letters were never lost. They call to you as I read over your pot every day and every night. Most days you are too busy to listen, but the tears your soul cries every night let me know you do hear me."

With a confused look on her face the princess said, "I'm sorry. I'm not sure I understand. You know about my letters, the ones I had when I was young? And why do you call out to me? And what are you doing with this gold?"

"My sweet child," the man said softly. "It has been so long since we last talked. It has been so long since you last read my letters. I wrote those letters to you. I am the one who calls out to you now. And this gold is your life, my daughter. Every day I stir and stir and wait for the imperfections to rise to the surface. I then scrape them off and cast them aside. Then I stare down into the pot to check for my reflection. As the gold purifies, I can see more and more of myself in you."

"You called me daughter?" the girl said with a puzzled look on her face.

"Oh, yes. You are Mine. You are My princess. You have been chosen to marry My Son at the great wedding one day. You will be His bride, His beloved. I do all of this to get you ready, My child, to get you ready for Him," the man said with an excited expectancy.

"Me?" The girl questioned. "I'm chosen? I'm loved? I'm a princess?" she said in sheer delight. Then suddenly a pain seared her heart and she felt her chest tighten. "Oh, but I don't qualify to be a princess. You don't know what I've done."

"Before the creation of the earth, I thought of you and I loved you. In My perfect timing I formed you in your mother's womb. I danced with you in the meadows and placed dreams in your heart. I have walked with you every step of your life. I have saved every tear you've ever cried. My heart broke with each sob that ever poured forth from your soul."

The man paused as a tear rolled down his cheek. "And yes, I do know what you've done. I know every secret in your heart. That's why I sent My Son to die in your place. But He did not succumb to death. He defeated death and rose again so that you could be forgiven and set free. All you have to do is give me the key to all those chains that bind your heart in hurt and hopelessness. I will release you from your bondage and sin. I will wipe your tears and fill your heart with My love."

"You really love me," she said. She reached into her pocket and retrieved a small metal object. It had grown rusty over the years from her many salty tears. The snake had loved to take this key, unlock the hurting parts of her heart, and remind her of how ugly, guilty, and unlovable she was.

Tears flowed from her eyes and splashed into the pot as she leaned over and dropped the old rusty key into the golden mixture. "Oh, Father, my King, my Redeemer, stir my pot and put me through whatever it takes to get me ready for Your Son. Take these chains that bind me and strip them from my heart. Never again will I let the snake deceive me into thinking I am worthless. Never again will I let him write his name across my heart. Lead me, Father. Refine me until you see Your reflection in me. Teach me, mold me, and make me into a bride fit for the most high Prince."

Suddenly she awoke. "No," she cried, "don't take the dream from me."

Then she remembered the letters. Quickly, she jumped out of bed and pulled the old, dusty box from underneath. She threw open the lid and gathered the letters into her arms. "I love You, Father! I love You," she cried. She lit a small candle beside her bed. As the warm glow of light flickered and danced around the small room, the words of comfort and reassurance filled her heart. These were love letters. Her love letters. From a Father to His child and from a Groom coming soon to claim His bride.

"Forever and ever only You will hold the key to my heart," the princess whispered through her joyous tears. She reached into the pocket of her gown to get the old key, but it was gone.

TIPS FOR GROUP LEADERS

This book was designed to cover eleven sessions. In your first session, it's helpful to start with a get–acquainted activity so the women get to know one another and feel comfortable in the group. Then, as the leader, give a general overview of the contents of the book. This will require that you read the first couple of chapters and at least glance over the rest of the book to become familiar with the material. Next, go over the guidelines for group meetings below and ask the women if there's anything else they'd like to add to these guidelines.

It will be helpful to hand out a schedule with the dates each chapter will be read and discussed. That way, if anyone has to miss a meeting, she'll know what the group will be studying the next week. The first meeting is also the time to take care of the business of purchasing books, if that hasn't already been done.

The second session will be a discussion of the study questions at the end of the introduction; the third session will cover chapter one, and so on.

If your group wants to complete the study in ten weeks, you may omit the get-acquainted session and discuss the study questions and the introduction in your first meeting. In this case you would want to make sure the women have purchased their books and read the introduction before the first session. This will work best for established groups in which group members already know one another.

The focus of the group meetings will be the discussion questions at the end of each chapter. If the group members want to, and time permits, you may also discuss journal questions or concepts found in the chapter. Your responsibility as the group leader is simply to facilitate discussion. Don't worry if you aren't a Bible scholar!

Encourage your group members to read the assigned chapter and answer the journal questions before coming to class. That way they'll get the most out of the study. However, if anyone is unable to complete the material, encourage her to come to the group meeting anyway. She will still get a lot out of the discussion, and she can catch up on her reading during the next week.

GUIDELINES FOR GROUP MEETINGS

The goal of the group is to support one another as the members allow God to transform their lives. To make everyone feel comfortable sharing deep personal hurts, stress that everything said is confidential and should not be shared outside the group. Also emphasize that it is not the purpose of the group to judge one another. The group should be a place of safety. Your group may wish to add other guidelines or goals.

If you have a particularly talkative group, you may not be able to complete all the discussion questions in a session. In that case, simply choose four or five that are the most relevant to your group; then discuss the other questions as time allows.

Be sensitive to the women in your group. No one has to share anything from her personal journal during group time unless she would like to. Encourage shy women to speak up by giving a little extra time between questions, but don't force anyone to talk. When they feel comfortable in the group, they will speak up.

Don't let any one woman dominate the discussion. If the group is going off on a tangent, redirect it to the topic at hand. If anyone is sharing unbiblical teachings, gently but firmly confront her and state the truth from Scripture.

You will want to end each session with prayer for some of the hurts or concerns shared in the group. Encourage the women to pray for each other during the week as well.

God bless you, my friend, as you lead your group of women on an exciting journey to healing and wholeness.

NOTES

CHAPTER ONE
Shame Is Satan's Signature; Love Is God's Reply

1. Portions of this chapter are adapted from chapter 3 of Lysa TerKeurst and Sharon Jaynes, *Seven Life Principles for Every Woman* (Chicago: Moody, 2001); and chapters 5 and 9 of Lysa TerKeurst, *Living Life on Purpose: Discovering God's Best for Your Life* (Chicago: Moody, 2000).

CHAPTER TWO
Despair Is Satan's Destiny; Joy Is God's Reply

1. Francis Frangipane, *The Three Battlegrounds: An In-depth View of the Three Arenas of Spiritual Warfare: The Mind, the Church and the Heavenly Places* (Cedar Rapids, Iowa: Arrow, 1989), 9.

2. *Life Application Study Bible,* NIV version (Wheaton, Ill., Tyndale; Grand Rapids: Zondervan, 1988), commentary, 1048.

3. Neil T. Anderson, *The Bondage Breaker* (Eugene, Oreg.: Harvest House, 1990), 23.

CHAPTER THREE
Fear Is Satan's Delight; Peace Is God's Reply

1. Linda Dillow, *Calm My Anxious Heart* (Colorado Springs: Nav-Press, 1998), 121–22.

2. Dr. Archibald Hart, *The Anxiety Cure* (Nashville: Word, 1999), 157.

3. Dillow, *Calm My Anxious Heart,* 123.

4. Oswald Chambers, *My Utmost for His Highest* (New York: Dodd, Mead, 1935), entry for May 23.

5. Hart, *The Anxiety Cure.*

6. Francis Frangipane, *The Three Battlegrounds: An In-depth View of the Three Arenas of Spiritual Warfare: The Mind, the Church and the Heavenly Places* (Cedar Rapids, Iowa: Arrow, 1989), 52.

CHAPTER FOUR
Discontentment Is Satan's Distraction; Patience Is God's Reply

1. Kay Arthur, *Lord Only You Can Change Me* (Sisters, Oreg.: Multnomah, 1995), 152.

2. James Patterson and Peter Kim, *The Day America Told the Truth* (New York: Prentice Hall, 1991); as quoted in *Discipleship Journal,* September–October 1991, 16.

3. Billy Graham, *Day by Day with Billy Graham,* comp. and ed. Joan Winmill Brown (Minneapolis: World Wide, 1976), devotion for September 23.

CHAPTER FIVE
Loneliness Is Satan's Trap; Kindness Is God's Reply

1. Max Lucado, *The Final Week of Jesus* (Sisters, Oreg.: Multnomah, 1994), 93–94.

2. Ibid., 82.

3. Brent Curtis and John Eldredge, *The Sacred Romance: Drawing Close to the Heart of God* (Nashville: Thomas Nelson, 1997), 87–88.

4. Nancy Leigh DeMoss, *Singled Out for Him* (Buchanan, Mich.: Life Action Ministries, 1998), 20.

5. Elizabeth Elliot, *Loneliness* (Nashville: Thomas Nelson, 1988), Dedication.

CHAPTER SEVEN
Doubt Is Satan's Whisper; Faithfulness Is God's Reply

1. H. E. Manning, quoted in Elisabeth Elliot, *Keep a Quiet Heart* (Ann Arbor, Mich.: Servant, 1995), 147.

2. *Life Application Study Bible,* NIV version (Wheaton, Ill., Tyndale; Grand Rapids: Zondervan, 1988), commentary on Psalm 77:1–12, page 987.

3. Elisabeth Elliot, *Loneliness* (Nashville: Thomas Nelson, 1988), 88–89.

4. Rebecca Manley Pippert, *Hope Has Its Reasons* (San Francisco: Harper & Row 1989), 119.

CHAPTER EIGHT
Bitterness Is Satan's Revenge; Gentleness Is God's Reply

1. Beth Nimmo and Darrell Scott, *Rachel's Tears: The Spiritual Journey of the Columbine Martyr Rachel Scott* (Nashville: Thomas Nelson, 2000), 91–92.

2. Ibid., dedication.

3. Ibid., 171–72.

4. Ibid., 175.

5. Ibid., 179.

CHAPTER NINE
Addiction Is Satan's Pleasure; Self-Control Is God's Reply

1. Dr. Alan Leshner, in Geoffrey Cowley, "New Ways to Stay Clean," *Newsweek,* 12 February 2001, 46.

2. Joann Condie, Licensed Professional Counselor with Focus on the Family, interview.

3. *The Life Application Study Bible,* NIV version (Wheaton, Ill.: Tyndale; Grand Rapids: Zondervan, 1988), commentary, page 2145.

4. Condie, interview.

5. Cowley, "New Ways to Stay Clean, *Newsweek,* 46.

CONCLUSION

1. Hannah Hurnard, *Hinds' Feet on High Places* (Wheaton, Ill.: Tyndale, 1975), 164.

2. Ibid., 236.

renewing the heart®
Truth and Grace for Daily Living

Welcome to a Special Place Just for Women

We hope you've enjoyed this book.
Renewing the Heart, a ministry of Focus on the Family,
is dedicated to equipping and encouraging women in all facets of their
lives. Through our weekly call-in radio program, our Web site, and a
variety of other outreaches, Renewing the Heart is a place to find
answers, gain support, and, most of all, know you're among friends.

How to Reach Us

For more information and additional resources, visit our Web site at
www.renewingtheheart.com. Here, you'll find articles, devotions,
and broadcast information on our weekly call-in radio program,
"Renewing the Heart," hosted by Janet Parshall.

To request any of these resources, call Focus on the Family at
800-A-FAMILY (800-232-6459). In Canada, call 800-661-9800.

You may also write us at:
Focus on the Family, Colorado Springs, CO 80995

In Canada, write to: Focus on the Family,
P.O. Box 9800, Stn. Terminal, Vancouver, B.C. V6B 4G3

To learn more about Focus on the Family or to find out if we have an
associate office in your country, please visit www.family.org.

We'd love to hear from you!

FOCUS ON THE FAMILY®

Welcome to the Family!

Whether you received this book as a gift, borrowed it from
a friend, or purchased it yourself, we're glad you read it! It's just
one of the many helpful, insightful, and encouraging
resources produced by Focus on the Family.

In fact, that's what Focus on the Family is all about—providing inspira-
tion, information, and biblically based advice to people in all stages of life.

It began in 1977 with the vision of one man, Dr. James Dobson, a licensed
psychologist and author of 16 best-selling books on marriage, parenting,
and family. Alarmed by the societal, political, and economic pressures
that were threatening the existence of the American family, Dr. Dobson
founded Focus on the Family with one employee—an assistant—
and a once-a-week radio broadcast, aired on only 36 stations.

Now an international organization, Focus on the Family is dedicated
to preserving Judeo-Christian values and strengthening the family
through more than 70 different ministries, including eight separate
daily radio broadcasts; television public service announcements;
10 publications; and a steady series of books and award-winning
films and videos for people of all ages and interests.

Recognizing the needs of, as well as the sacrifices and important
contributions made by, such diverse groups as educators, physicians,
attorneys, crisis pregnancy center staff, and single parents,
Focus on the Family offers specific outreaches to uphold and
minister to these individuals, too. And it's all done for one purpose,
and one purpose only: to encourage and strengthen individuals
and families through the life-changing message of Jesus Christ.

• • •

For more information about the ministry, or if we can be of help to your
family, simply write to Focus on the Family, Colorado Springs, CO 80995
or call 1-800-A-FAMILY (1-800-232-6459). Friends in Canada may write
Focus on the Family, P.O. Box 9800, Stn. Terminal, Vancouver, B.C. V6B 4G3.
or call 1-800-661-9800. Visit our Web site—www.family.org—
to learn more about Focus on the Family or to find out if
there is an associate office in your country.

We'd love to hear from you!

Other Exceptional Titles from Moody Press and Lysa TerKeurst!

Leading Women to the Heart of God

Leading Women to the Heart of God was developed with the leaders of women's ministry in mind. Packed with strategies and ideas to build a strong women's ministry, this book crosses denominational, racial and age boundaries as it incorporates perspectives from women of many diverse backgrounds all woven together with the common thread of their love for Jesus and passion for serving Him.

There are over 20 contributors including Michelle McKinney Hammond, Sharon Jaynes and Lisa Harper, all of whom are women who share their experience and knowledge.

ISBN: 0-8024-4920-4, Paperback, Women

Capture His Heart

If you've ever wished you could understand your husband better....this book is for you!

Men are fascinating. God made them that way. But many women find them frustrating and hard to figure out. Let me encourage you to put your own frustrations and disappointments aside and set out on a new adventure. A journey of understanding, acceptance and love for the heart of your beloved husband.

ISBN: 0-8024-4040-1, Paperback, Marriage

Capture Her Heart

If you've ever wished you could understand your wife better....this book is for you!

Statistics show that marriages inside and outside the church are failing at alarming rates. Having a great marriage takes time, creativity, and a willingness to understand the needs of the other person. Husbands, read this practical, quick read and fill up your marriage treasure chest with blessings from our Father!

ISBN: 0-8024-4041-X, Paperback, Marriage

Seven Life Principles for Every Woman

In society today, boundaries are blurred, roles are reversed and priorities perplex us. Do you feel like you need to bring your life into focus and achieve some sense of balance? Look no further!

"Sharon and Lysa have captured the heart of what it means to be a woman of God. With wisdom, warmth, and wit they present a compelling vision of the high calling that is ours as women. Their rich practical insights are solidly rooted in the Scripture and engagingly illustrated out of their own lives."
– Nancy Leigh DeMoss

ISBN: 0-8024-3398-7, Hardcover, Women (Book)
ISBN: 0-8024-3397-9, Paperback, Women (Bible Study)

Living Life on Purpose & The Life Planning Journal

Every women longs to live up to her full, God-given potential. But the hectic nature of life may leave you struggling just to keep your head above water. Fortunately, you can do more than simply survive. These two books can guide you in developing a Life Plan. More than just helping you get a better handle on your schedule, your Life Plan will allow you to enjoy a life that is truly well-lived.

0-8024-4195-5 *Living Life on Purpose*
0-8024-4196-3 *Life Planning Journal for Women*

Moody Press, a ministry of Moody Bible Institute,
is designed for education, evangelization, and edification.
If we may assist you in knowing more about Christ
and the Christian life, please write us without obligation:
Moody Press, c/o MLM, Chicago, Illinois 60610.